Keeping Company with Jamaica

Philip Sherlock

Ⓜ MACMILLAN
CARIBBEAN

First published 1984

Published by
Macmillan Publishers
London and Basingstoke
*Companies and representatives in Lagos, Zaria,
Manzini, Gaborone, Nairobi, Singapore, Hong Kong,
Delhi, Dublin, Auckland, Melbourne, Tokyo,
New York, Washington, Dallas.*

ISBN 0 333 37419 3

Printed in Hong Kong

To   Abe Issa
           John Pringle
           Ferdie Martin

           Pioneers of Tourism
           in Jamaica

Contents

Acknowledgements

The author wishes to express his warmest thanks to Mr Robert Britton of the Science Museum, Minnesota, for his invaluable help with developing the concept of what the guide should set out to achieve. If the reader agrees that the approach is a refreshing improvement on other guides then Robert Britton must share the credit for this.

The author is also grateful to Don Bryce, Herb Hiller, Ferdie Martin, Marcella Martinez and Joey Rafferty for their advice and assistance.

The author and publishers are grateful to George Allen & Unwin (Publishers) Ltd. for permission to reproduce two extracts from *Waters of the West* by Kenneth Pringle.

Whilst every effort has been made to trace and acknowledge copyright, in one case this has proved untraceable. The publishers apologise for any infringement of copyright and shall be glad to include the necessary correction in subsequent printings.

Photograph acknowledgements

The author and publishers wish to acknowledge, with thanks, the following photographic sources: J. Allan Cash; Barnaby's; Anne Bolt; Colour Library International; Stanley Gibbons; Jamaica Tourist Board; G.W. Lennox; The Photographer's Library; Pictor International; Picturepoint.
Cover photograph: Pictor International

The publishers have made every effort to trace the copyright holders, but if they have inadvertently overlooked any, they will be pleased to make the necessary arrangement at the first opportunity.

1 Jamaica and the Jamaicans

Welcome!

1 Keeping company with Jamaica

Jamaicans speak two languages, Jamaica Talk and English. Jamaica Talk is for family and friends and for communicating with other Jamaicans. It is also for abuse being rich in vivid imagery and devastating epithets.

In Jamaica Talk 'to keep company with someone' means much more than to accompany him or her. It means to be in tune with another person. It is warm, intimate. It tells of a journey to a destination and to the heart.

This book is for those who wish to keep company with Jamaica; who wish to combine sight-seeing with insight; who wish to make two journeys, one through a beautiful country and the other into the Jamaican way of life. It shows how to transform a visit into a discovery.

Discovery begins with arrival. A travel writer has described the process. Having passed through immigration and customs at the Norman Manley airport, which is on a narrow finger of land that almost encircles Kingston Harbour, he was on his way into the city by taxi.

Driving along a road choked with honking traffic, I suddenly saw a strange man, all arms and legs and very thin and wearing one of those incongruous caps, walking blithely along as if on a tight rope.

'What on earth is he doing there?' I asked the driver.

'Man,' he replied, 'he just walking along the white line. Why not?'

I knew I was back in Jamaica, the country of the individual who won't be a carbon copy of anyone. In Jamaica the barman who serves you talks to you on a

3

plane of total and unstudied equality. Some visitors don't like this, and my advice to them is that they should go somewhere else. Which would be a pity since they would miss one of the loveliest island countries in the world.

Jamaicans are characterised by individualism, and a tender yet fiercely possessive love of their country. The odds are that within an hour of your arrival a Jamaican, the taxi-driver maybe or the bell captain at the hotel, will ask 'How you like Jamaica?' The wise course is not to waste time explaining that you have just arrived but to declare, 'I have fallen in love with your country already.' This may well be true, for Jamaica takes possession of its visitors very quickly.

The first step in keeping company with Jamaica is to sweep away the clutter of clichés and slogans produced by the image-makers. Jamaicans resent stereotypes of themselves and their fellow West Indians as calypso singers and bongo drummers wearing fixed smiles and broad-rimmed hats. Struggling hard against poverty, they dislike talk about a 'tropical paradise'. Posters depicting palm trees, wide beaches and narrow bikinis lead them to insist, 'We're more than a beach, we're a country.' How much more sincere and adequate are the words the Elizabethan sailor John Sparke wrote more than three centuries ago, that Jamaica is 'a country marvelously sweet'. A hundred years earlier Columbus, the first European visitor to the Caribbean, wrote, 'It is the fairest isle that ever eyes beheld . . . and the mountains seem to touch the sky.'

The island challenges the visitor to get away from the beaten track and to explore its hidden valleys; to discover spectacular retreats like Cinchona and the coffee country round about Mavis Bank and Arntully; to go by canoe through the waterways of Swamp; to visit the Spas at Bath, Milk River and Sans Souci, all more efficacious than the waters of Baden-Baden; to explore caves and to scuba-dive along the offshore reefs.

The challenge is to explore oneself as well, to open up the mind and senses to a new physical and cultural environment. Thoreau would approve. 'Explore your own higher altitudes . . . Nay, be a Columbus to whole new continents and worlds within you, opening new channels not of trade but of thought.'

How is it that, though Jamaica is an island to which many tourists come, it is not a tourist island?

4

In part, it is because of the nature of the people and in part because of the mountains. The island is the top of a drowned mountain range. Between it and Cuba lies the Bartlett Trough, which is more than 20 000 feet deep in places. If the sea were drained away, Blue Mountain Peak, 7400 feet above sea-level, would almost rival Mount Everest.

The extraordinary thing is that the land sweeps upward so swiftly. The island is only a hundred and forty-six miles long and fifty-three miles across at the widest part. From Kingston to Port Antonio, as the crow flies, is only twenty miles. Yet that narrow space is packed tight with the highest peaks in the islands of the Commonwealth Caribbean: with Catherines Peak, Stoddards Peak, Half a Bottle, Corn Puss Gap and Blue Mountain Peak.

To get an unforgettable picture of the island, fly from Montego Bay to Kingston; or from Ocho Rios or Port Antonio; or from Kingston to Mandeville and Montego Bay. Try for a clear morning, before the clouds start gathering. From the plane you will see how the central range and the ridges and spurs that branch out laterally split Jamaica into an archipelago, with an encircled saucer of fertile land here, a confusion of hills there, and scattered pasturelands. Seeing the many divisions, it is easy to understand how it is that, though Jamaicans identify with Jamaica, each identifies also with his own parish (a St James man, a St Elizabeth woman, a Portlander and so on) and with a particular district or village where he still has 'family' or owns a share of the 'family land'.

The mountains mould the island's many faces. They account for the variations in elevation, climate, rainfall and soil. The misty valleys of the Rio Grande in Portland are lush wet tropics and, to the south, on the other side of the mountain range, is the gaunt cactus landscape of the Hellshire Hills just to the west of Kingston.

An hour's driving takes the visitor from wet tropics to dry; from hot lowlands to cool hill country; from the wind-cooled north coast to cold green pastures and 'the stunted pine trees of mountain Jamaica with strawberries and conifers'; from housing developments and estates to cattle country, smallholdings and mountain settlements.

Through these close-set contrasts Jamaica captures all the

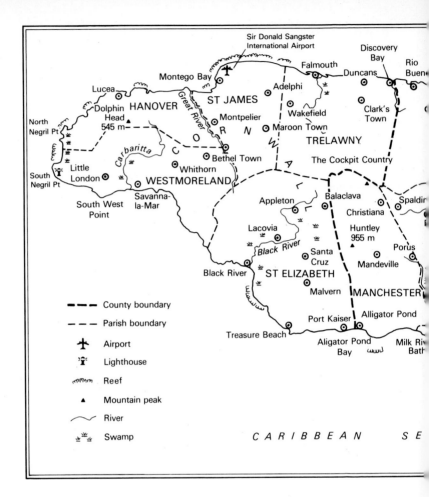

senses: sight, hearing, taste, smell and touch. Memory being the most lasting and precious part of any vacation, some sounds and scents bring back special occasions: evenings in a garden above Ocho Rios with the star-jasmine in flower; a road near Mandeville fragrant with orange blossoms; the pungent sweet-sour smell of a newly-harvested field of sugar-cane near Rose Hall; the scent of coffee being parched in the outside kitchen of a country cottage; the spicy tang of pimento; the smell of pork and chicken barbecued over pimento logs; fish being fried at wayside stalls; the turpentine-smell of ripe mangoes; the clamour of a country market; the shrill music of cicadas at sundown time; a mocking bird pouring out its heart from the

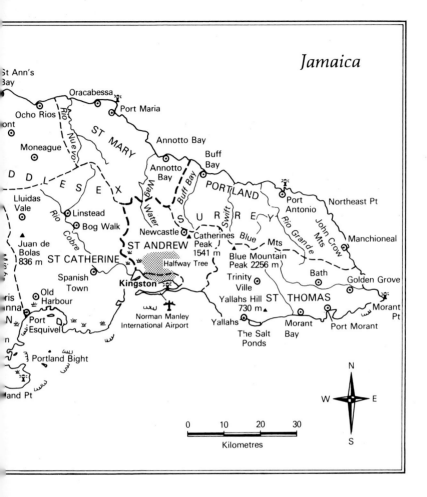

Jamaica

topmost branch of a poinciana tree; and in city and country village the sound of reggae, of Bob Marley's 'By the rivers of Babylon' and 'No Woman, nuh cry' and of his other songs which have touched the heart of the world.

There are other sounds and smells to be listed. The unmistakable smell of ganga or marijuana; the crowing of roosters that greet the dawn three hours or so before it is due; dogs that bark through the long hours of the night and donkeys that bray on the hour. These all have their place in Jamaica.

Opening our senses to the physical environment of land, sea and air, we find that the country has a rhythm of its own and that the landscape is not a splendid backdrop or stage setting, but an essential part of the Jamaican way of life. People and land are a harmony. Skin tones, gesture, language, music and dance repeat and recreate the rhythm to which life moves, relaxed yet at times intense, with its own pace, its own unique modes of expression. The Caribbean world breaks in upon us, a world of hubbub and laughter, of people who speak with the whole body, eyes and face, arms, shoulders, torso and hips, filling each word with drama.

But Jamaica is more than a glorious landscape. Keeping company with Jamaica involves finding out something about the Jamaican experience; learning how Jamaicans are grappling with unemployment; how they are trying to strengthen their economy and improve the standard of living of the people; how they are struggling to provide their children with a better future.

This book is written in the hope that the visitor will not allow the beauty of the land to blind him to something more significant, the emergence of a dynamic society of free people.

In the Blue Mountains

This means looking at another landscape, that of history. For a hundred and fifty years Jamaica was a slave and sugar plantation, ruled and owned by a small white society and inhabited by a large majority of African slaves, each of whom was bound by law to a particular estate. That period lasted from 1655, when the English took Jamaica from Spain, up to the year of emancipation, 1834. For a hundred years after that Jamaica was a Crown colony, ruled from London with a small powerful élite of white and brown people, and with a large majority of black people who were excluded from political power. In the years between 1944 and 1962 Jamaica moved from being a colony to becoming independent. A decisive step was taken in 1944 when the black majority was granted the vote and brought into the political process. In 1962 the island achieved independence.

In forty years – a short time in the life of a nation – Jamaicans have created a national identity, used their political power with

sophistication and good judgement, shown the ability to manage their affairs and are creating forms of artistic and cultural expression which have their roots in the indigenous and not in the imported. More than anything else Jamaicans ask their visitors to see how, out of a past of fire, suffering and neglect, their spirit has survived and is now expressing itself through the dynamism of a creative society.

Those visitors who understand this find it easy to relate to Jamaicans. They understand why Jamaicans object to being called 'natives'. The word recalls a colonial society in which there were the 'rulers', superiors from overseas, and the inferior 'natives'. They understand also that, whereas Americans express friendliness and acceptance of others by using first names at their first meeting, Jamaicans are more formal. In their history the use of the first name was often a mark of inferior status. One begins with 'Mr' or 'Miss' or 'Lady' or 'Sir' as a mark of respect and status. Once that has been established, the use of first names follows. By then it is a sign of acceptance and friendship.

For Jamaicans respond quickly to friendship. Many of them have relatives overseas, in the United States, Canada and England. They enjoy talking about other lands and people as well as about their own country. 'Man,' they will tell you, 'travel is the best education.' And perhaps one will quote the Jamaican proverb 'if crab nuh walk, him don't grow claw', which means 'if a crab doesn't move around he won't grow complete'.

2 The land, its plants and animals

Name, size, location

There is some confusion about the origin of the name 'Jamaica'. Although 'JAMAICA' is recorded as early as 1511, several early Spanish historians use the form 'XAYMACA', an Arawak word that possibly meant 'land of springs'. When Columbus discovered the island in 1494 he named it St Jago (Santiago). Fortunately the old name survived, linking the island with the ancient world of the American Indians.

Jamaica is the third largest of the fifty-one inhabited islands in the Caribbean archipelago. Cuba is largest, with 44 000 square miles, one-half the total land area. Haiti and the Dominican Republic share the second largest island, Hispaniola, which is 30 000 square miles in area. Jamaica has an area of 4400 square miles, and is a third larger than Puerto Rico, which comes fourth with 3400 square miles. The other forty-seven islands share the remaining 7000 square miles. Nowhere else in the Americas is there such imbalance in size between countries, and no other New World countries are affected so harshly by economies of scale.

The four large islands, the Greater Antilles, make up the western half of the archipelago. Jamaica lies just inside the rim, ninety miles south of eastern Cuba. It has considerable strategic value, for it is centrally placed. It is equidistant – five hundred miles – from Miami, San Juan and Colon, and it commands some of the chief sea-routes of the Caribbean. Its strategic value was even greater in the days of sailing ships, so much so that after the English took it from Spain in 1655 a Spanish diplomat

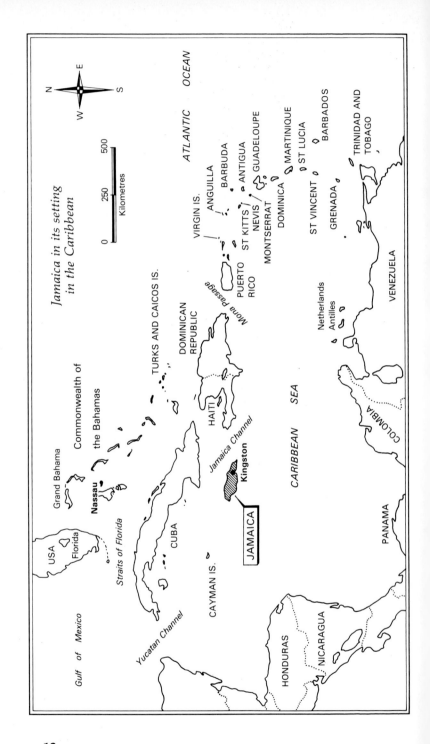

Jamaica in its setting in the Caribbean

described it as 'a dagger pointed at the soft underbelly of Spanish America'.

The population numbers two million, with a population density of 450 to the square mile. But the island is so mountainous that only one-half of it is cultivable, and there are large areas in the Cockpit Country and the Blue Mountains that are not habitable. It is more accurate to think of the population density as being about nine hundred to the cultivable square mile.

It is part of Jamaica's charm that it is not in the 'big island league', for large islands, like continents, are not collectible. They cannot be taken to one's heart and spiritually possessed, like middle-sized and small islands. Man's dream islands, his Utopias, have all been on a small scale.

The final word on size and on the way in which Jamaicans see their country belongs to Louise Bennett, known to all Jamaicans as Miss Lou. At the time when the island became independent, 6 August, 1962, she wrote a poem saying she hoped the world-map had been cautioned 'not to draw Jamaica small', and

We mus' tell map
We don't like we position,
Please kindly take we out o' sea
And draw we in de Ocean.

The face of the land

Geologically there are two Jamaicas, one older than the other. The older part is the eastern quarter of the island, which includes the parishes of Portland, St Thomas and St Andrew.

In the far distant past volcanic upheavals thrust this part above sea-level and, after a period of time, submerged it again. Through long ages marine polyps covered it with a blanket of limestone. There followed a series of upheavals which lifted a larger Jamaica above sea-level, with 3000 square miles of limestone-covered rock attached to the older portion.

This second series of upheavals propelled the land upward in stages, forming terraces and plateaux that range from 1500 to 3500 feet above sea-level. Some of the escarpments are spectacular. At Lovers Leap, west of Alligator Pond on the

13

south coast, the land rises abruptly 1600 feet above the sea. On the north coast, inland from Ocho Rios, is the famous Fern Gully, a three-mile water course that runs from the plateau around Hopewell down the escarpment to the coast.

Its thick limestone blanket gave Jamaica its bauxite. Water that contains even a weak solution of acids can dissolve limestone. Through countless millennia the rain dissolved vast quantities of the limestone, leaving the 'red earth' that is so characteristic of central and western Jamaica. The red earth contains iron and bauxite, the ore from which aluminium is made.

Rafting on the Martha Brae River, near Falmouth

Water, a persistent sculptor, wrought other marvels. It produced the Cave River and Hectors River, which rise and then disappear, and the Y.S. River which disappears and then reappears to join the Black River in St Elizabeth. It gouged out sink holes and carved underground channels through which hidden streams drain away into deep lagoons, such as the lagoon at the Green Grotto on the road from Discovery Bay to Runaway Bay. It fashioned a maze of subterranean reservoirs and tunnels, with lakes that appear periodically at Moneague and at Newmarket in Westmoreland. It hollowed out caves such as those in the Dry Harbour mountains, and on the Hopewell and Cave Valley estates.

In a display of power, nature created the almost impenetrable confusion of the Cockpit Country and the John Crow mountains. Describing these mountains that break the power of the north-east trade winds on the Portland coast, the Jamaican novelist, John Hearne, writes: 'There are areas known in any one generation to perhaps half a dozen men.... In some parts a man could fall a long way down the sink-hole.... If you move a yard off the paths you need a machete, and trying to cut your way through a tangle of fairy bamboo makes as much sense as running into a barbed wire fence....'

Underground streams and subterranean reservoirs mean a lack of surface water. Jamaicans have found ways of surviving through humdrum routines. In the pastures they have made circular dew-ponds which have provided the cattle with water save in times of extreme drought. As a necessary part of each cottage and house they have built tanks and erected make-shift cisterns for storing water. If the standpipe that brought water from the large public tanks was far away, women and children carried buckets and tins of water on their heads to their homes.

An island of contrasts

Jamaica is an island of contrasts packed close in a small space. Wet Jamaica is in the north-east, the area of the John Crow mountains and the Blue Mountain range. Kenneth Pringle, in a forgotten book, *Waters of the West*, describes what this part of mountain Jamaica is like.

15

The part allotted to Corbett and myself was to proceed up to the Corn Puss Gap and build a hut for the first night's camp. The four foot track wound deviously about the hills above the Rio Grande which all the way sounded louder as it narrowed.... The Corn Puss Gap is so called, according to the bushmen, because the Maroons once salted (corned) a wild cat in that pass....

From a flat grass piece just above the knoll you can see north over the dark green irregular ranges as far as the blue arc of water which is Port Antonio and south over the cultivated mellow plains of St Thomas to the coast at Morant Bay.

We built there a tall hut flanked with poles and provided with a raised floor of poles. We wove a fresh green roof of thatch-palm pleated so close that rain could not penetrate. Then we lit a fire under another shelter outside and prepared an evening meal of fried mullet and coco and a great shut-pan of tea. Murray and Jackson and Johnson arrived in time to smell it and ascend with joyous cries. The bushmen were in high spirits because of the remarkably fine weather – 'Backra luck' they called it. But Backra's luck did not hold for long.

Sunset that evening was the first sign we had of trouble. The John Crows, rising sheer above us, vanished in a sombre watery purple haze. The voices of those a few feet away sounded like voices heard under water. If one went out, one was soaked with damp in a few minutes. Yet when we turned in, it had not yet begun to rain. It started about midnight, quietly, a long sigh like the breaking of a wave, and streamed down in a steady sheet. It did not stop, although it lightened from time to time, for four days.

This is old Jamaica, one which Jamaicans and their guests will wish to explore. There the environment has hardly been disturbed. Yet this was never our environment, for we are imported people living in a largely imported environment. In this respect we are like many other New World people. As the population grew the fields and plantations spread, destroying the natural vegetation. This in turn meant the disappearance of indigenous animals like the iguana and the Indian cony, which was 'of a distasteful shape like an overgrown rat'.

Some of the old forest trees remain; mahogany, cedar, bullet-wood which blunts the sharpest nail, mahoe; but they are now sadly diminished. The imported plants flourish as if this has always been their home.

The importation of plants started when Arawak Indians from the basin of the Orinoco began settling in the Caribbean islands two thousand years before the birth of Christ. They took with them their basic crops, cassava and maize, their sacred tobacco, and possibly other plants such as pineapples and sour-sop. But they were not meat-eaters. They lived off fish and shellfish. The rubbish heaps outside their village sites showed that they consumed large quantities of molluscs.

The second wave of importation started with the Spanish settlement of the island. What a whirlwind of change it was,

A typically colourful wayside stall

produced by a new technology based on steel, gunpowder, the compass, quadrant and sails. The importations included sugar-cane, citrus, cattle, swine and horses. Within the space of a century and a half the Arawaks were swept away by this hurricane.

The third great wave of importation of plants started in the late eighteenth century when the slave population of the sugar islands, Jamaica, Barbados, Antigua and St Kitts, were being wiped out by famine. This was the period of Bligh, the mutiny on the *Bounty* and the arrival in Jamaica of Bligh's second ship, the *Providence*, with seven hundred breadfruit trees and many other plants; the time of Dr Clarke, first government botanist, who brought in the ackee tree from West Africa in 1778; the time of Admiral Rodney and Captain Marshall who captured a French ship taking mango plants from Mauritius to the West Indies in 1782 and had the plants re-routed to Jamaica; and the time of a host of other introductions, such as yams, okra, coffee and guinea grass from Africa.

With the food-bearing trees came also some of the chief flowering trees and shrubs of Jamaica; the allamanda, bougainvillaea, oleander, spathodea, and royal poinciana or flamboyant.

No serpent in the garden

Jamaica has no wild animals – no jaguars, pumas, no poisonous snakes. The yellow snake, which was harmless, has dis-appeared. The mongoose helped to wipe it out, so now the only wild animal the visitor is likely to see is the mongoose himself – crossing a country road, thin, tawny, furtive as a weasel. The lizards are small and harmless, though most Jamaicans recoil from them as from a fierce dragon. The green lizards overcome the colour problem by changing from emerald green to near black, as circumstances require. When courting, the male blows out a splendidly-coloured throat-fan, lemon-yellow, brown, orange, his silent rendering of the wolf-whistle. Quite harmless, but most disliked of all, is the 'croaking lizard' which gets its name from the noise it makes. The folk say, 'When croakin' lizard bawl, sign of rain comin'.'

The Doctor Bird, Jamaica's national bird

The birds of Jamaica

Look out for the flying jewels that we call humming birds.
There are four varieties in the island: a Mango Hummer, known
in Haiti as 'black magic' because a dried powder from its body is
an effective love potion; the minute Bee Hummer, of dark
green; the Vervain, one of the world's smallest birds; and the
Doctor, known also as Streamer-Tail, Long-Tail or Scissors-
Tail. The male is a glittering green with the top of the head and
crest black. This 'black top hat' earns the bird his name, because
in earlier years a doctor's professional dress included a black top

19

hat. The elongated tail feathers of the male form a lovely pair of streamers, often twice the length of the body. The wing and under-tail coverts appear deep violet or blue-black. This hummer, which is found only in the island, is depicted on the Jamaica dollar bill as the national bird.

The Mocking Bird or Jamaica Nightingale delights in singing from the topmost twig of a tall tree in the morning and at sunset. He sings at all seasons and, because he seems at times to imitate the notes of other birds, he is called the Mocking Bird. Gosse, in his classic study of the *Birds of Jamaica*, describes him as 'bold and forward in his manners, inviting rather than avoiding notice, of striking though not showy colours'. The colouring is silver-grey, with large white wing patches and with the outermost feathers of the wing white.

The Jamaica Canary is a finch of the same family as the many quits that feed on the lawns and are prepared to join a visitor at the breakfast table. But he is much more vivid than the Black-face and Yellow-face Grass Quits, more jewel-like even than the Orange Quit or 'Long mout Quit' with its breast of deep chestnut red and (if a male) with violet-blue colouring. The upper parts are a bright olive-yellow, the forehead and crown a bright orange, the underparts a bright yellow. The bill is dull yellow with a dark tip on the lower mandible; altogether an enchanting little bird.

The John Crow is one of the first birds you will see, its plumage black as a parson's coat. It is an expert glider and most graceful in flight, but downright repulsive on land with its funereal appearance and bald red head. It is said that an Irish parson, the Reverend John Crow, preached a very unpopular sermon in Port Royal in the early buccaneering days. The bird's appearance reminded his audience of the priest so they gave it his name in derision. It is a good story but not supported by any evidence. Occasionally there is an albino John Crow; he is known as John Crow Parson or John Crow Headman, being white. There is a Jamaican proverb that warns 'Every John Crow thinks his pickney white' or, your own children (or other possessions) are the best in the world.

The Petchary, small bird of the tyrant flycatcher family, gets his name from his fierce, ceaseless shrieks. If you see a little ball of grey feathers shrieking 'pecheery-pecheery-pecheery' and dive-bombing a John Crow, you will know that you are looking at a petchary. He usually arrives in the island in May.

The Banana Quit, on the other hand, is prepared to share breakfast with you. In Jamaica he has several names – Beany Bird, Bessie Coban and John Croppie. He loves sugar and bananas. Offer him some and he will make himself at home on your table, sometimes too much so. There are a number of other quits, one of the most common being the Grass Quit, a counterpart of the Jamaica Sparrow for cheekiness.

Commonly seen also are the Hopping Dick, or Jumping Dick, a thrush which hops and jumps his way across the garden, and the Ground Doves that feed on the ground. They are safe from boys with sling shots, because to shoot a 'duppy bird' brings disaster, even death. 'Duppy' is Jamaican for 'jumbie' or 'ghost'.

The Rocklands Bird Sanctuary at Anchovy in the hills above Montego Bay should be high on any list of places to be visited in Jamaica.

Reading list

Gardens and gardening

Caribbean Gardening, by Aimee Webster: distributed by Sangsters Bookstores: 'a complete guide to growing the tropic's best-loved trees, shrubs, annuals and pot plants'.
Gardens of Jamaica, by Alan Eyre; an account of the historic gardens of the island, including Hope Gardens, Castleton, Cinchona and Bath.

Birds

Some of the two hundred birds of Jamaica are described in these books:
Bird Watching in Jamaica by May Jeffrey-Smith
Birds of Jamaica, by Lady Taylor

Birds of the West Indies, by James Bond; a comprehensive work, published in 1936. This was followed by his *Field Guide to Birds of the West Indies*, published in 1947.

Works of reference

The Flora of Jamaica, by Adams, the standard work, thorough and scientific.

Natural history

From the period of the Spanish settlement of Jamaica and on through the British colonial period notable work was done on the flora and fauna of Jamaica. The great classics include *A Voyage to the Islands Madera, Barbados, Nieves, St Christophers and Jamaica* ... by Hans Sloane (1707 and 1725). Sloane's collection of the plants of Jamaica formed the nucleus of the collections in the British Museum of Natural History.

A Civil and Natural History of Jamaica by Patrick Browne, 1756. Second edition, without engravings, 1789.

History of Jamaica by Edward Long: 3 volumes, 1774.

A Naturalist's Sojourn in Jamaica, and *Birds of Jamaica*, both by Philip Gosse.

Report on the Geology of Jamaica, by Sawkins.

Flora of Jamaica, by Fawcett and Rendle. Fawcett was Director of the island's Botanical Gardens from 1886-1898.

3 The economy: bauxite and manufacturing

The money earners

The nation's chief money earners are agriculture, mining and quarrying, manufacturing and tourism.

Statistics about these sectors, their performance and the overall economy are published annually by a Government organisation, the National Planning Agency, 39–41 Barbados Avenue, Kingston 5 (tel: (809)-926-1480).

The figures for 1981 showed increases in the Gross Domestic Product, in the number of jobs available in the commercial sector, in the output of skilled and semiskilled manpower and an overall increase in trade.

A vulnerable economy

Jamaica seeks to stand on its own feet, but its development efforts are often hampered, even frustrated, by events beyond its control. The story is the same in many of the Caribbean islands. They are small. Their resources are limited. They depend on imported petroleum for energy, and the escalation of oil prices has been disastrous. Their exports of sugar and other agricultural commodities earn less because the markets are depressed. The population is also increasing too quickly.

The problem of population growth

One of the great success stories of Jamaica – and one not told often enough – is the control that public health authorities have gained over the killers of the last century: typhoid, malaria, smallpox, tuberculosis, dysentery. Cleaning up the water supply, eradicating hookworm, improving sanitation and public education have brought the mortality rate down. Seventy years ago the life expectancy of a Jamaican was thirty-seven years; today it is sixty years. In 1930 the infant mortality rate was 32.2 per thousand of live births; in 1979 it was down to 12.4 per thousand.

Bauxite

More than a century ago a Government geologist, Sawkins, reported that bauxite was present in the red earth, but no one was interested. Hans Oersted, a Danish chemist, had produced aluminium in 1825, but not until 1886 had Charles Hall of the United States and Paul Herault of France invented, quite independently of each other, an inexpensive method of making

Digging and loading bauxite

aluminium. Even after commercial production started, however, Sawkins's report was neglected.

By the 1930's world demand for aluminium had risen prodigiously and a bauxite rush was on, but not in Jamaica. Not until 1942 did Jamaicans discover that they were living on one of the world's largest deposits of bauxite. Surveys made in the 1960's showed that the deposits of commercial bauxite exceeded 600 million tonnes.

The discovery of bauxite in the 1940's was made by chance. A Kingston merchant and weekend farmer, Sir Alfred Da Costa, was puzzled by the poor yields he was getting from crops planted on parts of his estate at Crescent Park in St Ann. Analysis showed that the soil contained almost fifty per cent alumina. Thereupon he started negotiations that took Jamaica into the ranks of bauxite-producing countries. Reynolds Jamaica Mines recorded Sir Alfred's discovery on a plaque by the side of the Moneague-Kingston main road, near the Crescent Park Great House, about four miles east of Moneague.

By 1950 three alumina companies were at work in Jamaica: Reynolds Jamaica Mines, the Kaiser Bauxite Company and Alumina Jamaica, at the time a wholly-owned subsidiary of the Alumina Company of Canada, Alcan. They bought up large areas of land in central Jamaica, so as to safeguard their supplies, and started mining operations. Since much of the land had been used for cattle-rearing, the Government required that it should be kept in production until it was needed for mining. It required also that the topsoil should be replaced where land had been mined and that a programme of land-rehabilitation should be undertaken.

There are three stages in the production of aluminium. First, the topsoil is stripped away and the ore loaded on to trucks and taken to a central place for dry storage. Next, the bauxite is reduced to a chalky-looking white powder, alumina. Finally, the alumina is smelted and made into aluminium. It takes about three hundred pounds of bauxite to produce one hundred pounds of alumina. This in turn yields fifty-four pounds of aluminium.

Alumina Jamaica (ALJAM) pioneered the industry by building two plants to process the bauxite into alumina in Jamaica, the Kirkvine Works near Kendal and the Ewarton Works on the Ewarton-Kingston road. The company transports the alumina to a deep-water harbour which it built near Old Harbour, Port Esquivel, named after the first Spanish governor of the island.

The other companies decided to ship the ore to the United States for processing. Reynolds Jamaica Mines built an overhead bucket-trolley line, six miles long, to carry the bauxite from the company's Belmont plant near Moneague to its storage building and the deep-water pier on the western side of the bay at Ocho Rios. A sign marks the place, but the rust-coloured layer of dust that covers the building and smothers the nearby vegetation identifies the place much more loudly. The Kaiser Bauxite Company built a terminal on the south coast at Port Kaiser, and another on the north coast at Discovery Bay and laid down a railway thirteen miles long from Tobolski near Brown's Town to its dry storage building beside the bay. This is linked to the pier by a conveyor which runs under the motorway, and which can load thirty-eight thousand tonnes on to a ship in ten hours. Ships approach the pier by a channel forty feet deep and four hundred feet wide, made by blasting away a part of the offshore reef.

There are now five companies mining bauxite in Jamaica: Alcan, Reynolds Jamaica Mines, Kaiser, Alpart and Alcoa. They all pay royalties to the Government of Jamaica. In 1980 the bauxite and alumina industry provided about seventy-two per cent of total commodity export earnings and about twenty-three per cent of Central Government revenues. Then the world-wide recession pulled the rug out from under the industry, which was Jamaica's main source of foreign exchange, and left the island in trouble.

The bauxite companies made massive investments in Jamaica, and followed a liberal public-spirited policy. They knew that open-face mining leaves great scarlet gashes in green pastures, and that many Jamaicans were upset at the sight of monstrous bull-dozers tearing up the fields and at the thought of the earth of their country being carried off to foreign parts. But Jamaicans realised that the impact was not wholly one of extraction. They found satisfaction in the creation of deep-water harbours, roads and railways; in the replacing of the topsoil and the rehabilitation of the land; in afforestation; the rearing of beef-cattle; the provision of employment and a greatly increased flow of money. They valued the introduction of more sophisticated labour-relations than prevailed in the days when Jamaica's economy was wholly agricultural, and they found satisfaction in having modern technology in their country. They knew, also, that Jamaicans held positions of leadership in the industry, and that the companies respected and listened to the Government.

Visitors from large countries know how the economies of their own countries are hurt by a slow-down. They will understand how it hurts small countries that have no options.

Other mining operations

Gypsum is mined in the mountains just east of Kingston harbour. There are plans for expanding this as the base for a viable gypsum board industry. In addition, deposits of marble, peat and clay are being investigated.

27

Manufacturing

Jamaica is not in a position to choose between agriculture and industry. It has to improve and expand agricultural production for export and for greater self-sufficiency, and at the same time to expand agri-industry and light industry. It also has to find new markets and expand existing ones.

One answer to being small was to get together with other countries. In the late 1960's Jamaica, in partnership with other countries of the Commonwealth Caribbean, established a Caribbean Development Bank and a Caribbean Free Trade Area (CARIFTA) which later became the Caribbean Economic Community (CARICOM). This provided member countries with a much larger market in the Caribbean. At the same time, Jamaica and the other newly-independent countries established embassies and trading missions in North America and Western Europe, set about expanding their markets and provided incentives to attract investments from overseas. Jamaica is currently promoting investment in such manufacturing areas as garments, textiles, electronics, furniture, footwear, alcoholic beverages, chemicals and plastics, food-processing, handicrafts and pharmaceuticals. Investments in manufacturing industries may qualify for development and tax incentives. Encouragement is provided for production geared towards export and labour-intensive methods.

Under Industrial Incentives legislation various types of manufacturing enterprises qualify for tax holidays, the length of the period running from five to ten years. Those industries which are capital-intensive, the capital investment being not less than $9.5 million, may be granted a tax holiday for ten years.

The Caribbean Basin Initiative

Jamaica, like practically all the Caribbean island countries, is searching desperately for new or expanding markets, for foreign investment and for ways of increasing its productivity. The Caribbean Basin Initiative of the United States brought new hope. The heart of that programme is the provision for a one-way free trade area which allows certain products of the Caribbean

Basin countries to enter the United States free of customs duties for a twelve year period. The Bill, which became law in 1983, establishes a Generalised System of Preferences by which manufactured goods from eligible countries are allowed duty-free access to United States markets. There are about 2800 products currently eligible for GSP treatment. Jamaica benefits from being one of the eligible countries and has Most Favoured Nation status.

Supermarkets and boutiques

To get a quick picture of what Jamaica is producing from raw materials that are available pay a visit to a supermarket or to some of the many boutiques in the cities. Pay a visit also to plantations and sugar-factories: to Appleton to see how sugar and rum are made; to Prospect with its pimento trees; to Brimmer Hall to see how bananas and coconuts are cultivated; to any of the other plantations for which tours are advertised in the tourist resorts.

Every supermarket carries a variety of Jamaica rums, ranging from light to heavy, from white to amber to dark. All rums are aged and bottled under Government supervision, the average time in cask being five years. There is also a liqueur-type rum, produced by Wray & Nephew, which is fifteen years old. Visitors should approach with great caution the new white proof rum sold in bars, locally known as 'cow-neck' or as 'rude to parents'.

The best-known liqueurs include Tia Maria, Rumona and Pimento Dram, a special favourite at Christmas time and a pleasant remedy for stomach-ache. Look out also for a group of 'old Jamaica' award-winning and attractively packaged liqueurs, such as wild orange and coffee, produced by Dr Ian Sangster.

The shelves are laden with fruit-juices, jellies, marmalades and nectars, including such exotics as mango, papaya and tamarind. The processed foods include some excellent local soups, pepperpot, pumpkin, red peas and pigeon peas. Sauces abound, many of them fiery, so a drop or two will suffice. Best known of all, and a gourmet's item, is the well-loved Picka-

*The beautiful hand-dyed material known locally
as Carabatik*

Peppa sauce, richer and superior in flavour to any Worcester sauce. Nearby are various brands of coffee, some specially packaged in air-tight tins for export. And, of course, there are cigars. Royal Jamaica won the 1969 and 1971 Brussels Gold Medal for making the finest handmade cigars in the world.

The boutiques and specialty shops carry garments designed and made in Jamaica, attractive fabrics, jewellery, cosmetics and perfumes. Designer clothing and jewellery are among the 'best buys' in Jamaica. One of the interesting perfumes is Khus-Khus, made from the fragrant roots of the khus-khus grass. For generations Jamaica housewives put little bundles of the root in their linen cupboards amongst their sheets and towels, in the way that French and English housewives used lavender.

Include visits to the Kingston Crafts Market, the Montego Bay Crafts Market, which has more than two hundred stalls crowded with straw goods, fabrics and carvings, and the attractive Dunns River Park.

Most of these enterprises are new. Up to the 1950's Jamaica manufactured a very limited range of goods. By the 1970's the change was evident. I recall going into a supermarket in Ocho Rios and talking with the shopkeeper, who pointed to jar after jar of preserves, bottle after bottle of sauces and to tins of fruit juices, saying, 'See that label? Product of Jamaica. That's a good name, man. The country is advancing, coming up in the world.'

But the mood has changed. The owner of a boutique in one of the resort areas said, 'We worked hard, we built up a good business, but we have so little foreign exchange, our money has lost value, prices are high, and what kind of a future is there for the children?'

Many books about Jamaica and Jamaicans speak about an identity problem: that Jamaicans are people in search of an identity. Jamaicans know who they are. Their concern is not about identity but about security. The range of manufactured goods tells of the effort they have made. The faces show concern about the future.

The best furniture-making establishments are in Kingston and Montego Bay. The furniture industry, one of the oldest in the island, was established generations ago when owners of sugar estates brought out artisans and cabinet-makers from England to supervise the making of carts and mills for the estates and of fine furniture for the Great Houses. Beautifully carved four poster beds, of richly textured Jamaica mahogany, wardrobes, Windsor chairs and dining tables with elaborately-carved bases were the pride of the Great Houses. Some examples may be seen in Devon House in Kingston. Today Jamaican furniture finds a market in other Caribbean countries and in North America.

There has also been an extraordinary flowering of folk-art in straw-goods, carvings and sculpture, ornaments from shells and bamboo, and ceramics. Traditionally Jamaicans are a basket-weaving rather than a pottery-making folk; parts of the island are known for their fine work in straw. From parts of northern

The strawmarket in Kingston

St Catherine come 'jippi-jappa' hats, beautifully woven from fine strips of palm-leaf in the style of Panama hats. The straw, and the hat, are named after the town of Jipijapa in Ecuador. Today handsome ladies' bags are made'from this straw and from the coarser thatch palm, for which southern St Elizabeth is well known. In times past, straw hats were called trash hats, or thatch hats, or 'wha-fe-de' (what-to-do?) hats, a fun way of saying, 'This is the best I can afford'.

What is astonishing is the range of goods now being produced by the people. This is in part a result of pioneering work done by Jamaica Welfare, now the Social Development Commission; by some local organisations like MONEX and Caribcraft; by pioneer entrepreneurs and by Government-supported training centres. Tourism has provided the stimulus of a market and of direct contact between makers and buyers. The Kingston Crafts Market at the western end of Harbour Street, the Montego Bay Crafts Market, the Ocho Rios Craft Market with two hundred stalls for the display of work in straw, fabrics, wood and bamboo, and countless wayside stalls throughout the island bring visitor, producer and artist face to face. Questions about the work on display are welcome. Bargaining is part of the process of buying. Words of appreciation are always valued.

4 Agriculture – a way of life

My own piece of rockstone

Agriculture affects all Jamaica. About seventy-five per cent of the labour force is employed in some branch of agriculture as compared with eighteen per cent in manufacturing, six per cent in construction and one per cent in mining and quarrying.

The numbers give some idea of quantity but in Jamaica agriculture has to do with dreams as well as with cash, with a man's self-image and role in society as well as with ploughing and hoeing, with emotions and values as well as with processing and marketing produce. It is both a system of production and a way of life.

Even in these times of urban sprawl the Jamaican dream is still, for many, land and a house. There is a steady movement of people and of produce from town to country and back again. Families remember how grandfather rented an acre of hillside land from the estate owner, planted it out and was evicted while the yams and sweet potatoes were still in the ground. If they cannot buy they will rent, but ownership means security and freedom from control. The distrust is there even when the Government is the landlord. 'They won't sell it,' the peasant reasons, 'but they will rent it to we because they want to control we.' Every landless Jamaican dreams of the day when he will own what he affectionately calls 'his own little piece of rockstone'.

Cinnamon Hill, an old plantation house that once belonged to the family of Elizabeth Barrett Browning

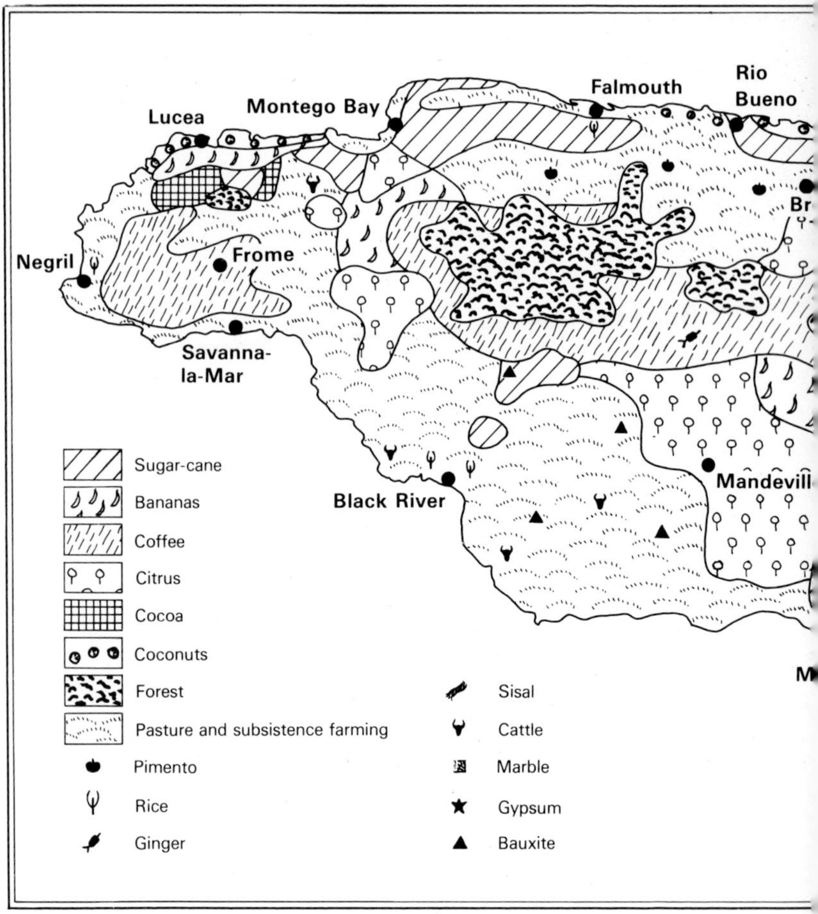

Lucea
Montego Bay
Falmouth
Rio Bueno
Negril
Frome
Savanna-la-Mar
Black River
Mandevill
Sugar-cane
Bananas
Coffee
Citrus
Cocoa
Coconuts
Forest
Pasture and subsistence farming
Pimento
Rice
Ginger
Sisal
Cattle
Marble
Gypsum
Bauxite

Land use and land distribution

Jamaica grows a variety of crops because of the differences in the elevation, temperature, climate and soils. The map shows how the land is used and how particular crops grow in specific areas.

The plains and the mountains made possible the development of two systems of agriculture. One is based on large holdings of land which produce crops for export and some food for the home market, and the other is based on smallholdings, which

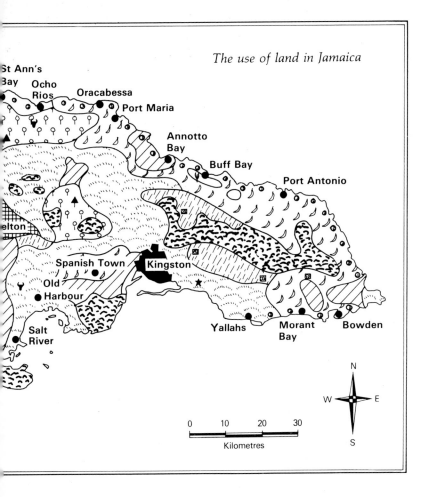

The use of land in Jamaica

provide some surplus for export and a large part of the local food supply.

History determined that the dual system should reflect the two societies which shared the island for nearly three centuries, one white and privileged, holding large tracts of land, the other black, exploited and without access to political power. Today independent Jamaica has established a national identity, and insists on equality of opportunity and freedom. The two systems of agriculture will continue, but now they mirror one society.

37

The estate system

The older system is that of plantation or estate agriculture, in which large holdings of land and a large labour force formed a unit for mass-producing one or two crops for export. The oldest sugar estate belt in Jamaica lies between Montego Bay and Falmouth. The story is written in the landscape, in the fields of sugar-cane that still flourish and in the ruins of old estates, such as the Running Gut Estate on the Rose Hall golf course. The Rose Hall Great House, Rose Hall Estate, Cinnamon Hill where the Barrett Family lived, and Cinnamon Hill Estate awaken echoes of the days when sugar was king.

Many Great Houses are in disrepair or in ruins. The planter families have disappeared. The production system based on free masters and black bondsmen was destroyed in 1834, the date of emancipation. A visit to any sugar estate within easy reach, however, will show that the basic patterns of cultivation and of production remain the same. Sugar-cane is a crop that is most efficiently cultivated in large units on flat or gently rolling land. Sugar is a manufactured product, in which the juice is extracted from the cane, boiled, converted to sugar and refined. The fields have to be within easy reach of the factory because the juice must be extracted within a day or two of the harvesting of the cane. Otherwise, the juice ferments and the crop is lost.

The smallholdings

The smallholding system came later. It grew out of the estate system, which was based on a large labour force of African people. This labour force had to be fed. The more the cane-fields spread, the more the demand for labour increased; the larger the labour force the greater the demand for food, for salted and pickled fish, flour and cornmeal from Boston and Savannah and Charleston, as well as for other plantation supplies. The estates allotted patches of 'hillside land' or 'mountain land' to the slaves for growing 'breadkind', yams, sweet potatoes and the like. When war interrupted the lifelines from North America, or when hurricanes destroyed the provision grounds, blacks died from starvation. More than fifteen thousand people were lost in this way between 1780 and 1787.

Immediately after emancipation many of the 'new frees' set off into the hills to found free villages of their own, and to lay out provision grounds, often with the help of Baptist and Methodist missionaries. In this way Jamaica gained its black peasantry, its system of smallholdings and some of its most important crops, among them the banana.

Bananas – and the smallholder

Banana cultivation contrasts sharply with that of sugar-cane. The banana tree is equally at home on a smallholding, a patch or a plantation. It is fast-growing, requires little care, calls neither for special equipment nor a factory. It has only to be ripened to be enjoyed as a fruit. The banana is packed full of such essential minerals as potassium, calcium and iron, and is almost wholly alkaline. The peasant knew nothing of the nutritional details, but he knew that green and ripe bananas added greatly to his food supply and earned him a quick return on his labour.

Country market and higgler women

Statistics and diagrams take on flesh and blood in country markets, and where better can a visitor see, pictured before him, the produce of the land and the way of life of rural Jamaica?

The hubbub begins on Friday afternoon. Buses packed to capacity with passengers and produce plough through the narrow streets, scattering pedestrians as a strong breeze scatters leaves.

By Saturday morning the market is in full swing. A few of the traders are men: there are some butchers in white aprons at their stalls; two or three men with machetes standing by a truck laden with green water-coconuts; a man selling 'wet sugar' and

A market scene

jackass-rope, a long twist of tobacco leaves, half an inch in diameter, prepared for smoking and sold by the inch; a man with a brightly-painted hand cart with a large block of ice and bottles of thick sweet syrup, yellow, red, purple, green. This is really a women's world, however, dominated by 'higglers', a name applied to the seller of any kind of small produce and goods. Many of them are substantial in build and are also women of substance. Mrs Smith, presiding over a heap of yellow yams and sweet potatoes, has a daughter studying at university; Aunt Liz, with her scale and calalu, cucumbers tomatoes and okra, has a son working in Toronto. They carry on their business with an easy air of authority, tough yet generous, bred to hardship, yet gentle. Their authority extends far beyond the market for, however assertive the men may be, the mother and grandmother are dominant in rural Jamaica, and the society of which they form a part is in many respects matriarchal.

The higgler women have a long history of itinerant trading. Over the generations, on foot or astride a donkey, they have established an internal marketing system which has moved the goods from remote holdings, by hillside tracks and by dirt roads, to villages and towns. Trading is in their blood. They are intrepid entrepreneurs, undaunted by circumstances, eager to grasp at opportunities. From head-carrying, donkeys and hampers they moved to cars and buses and to markets beyond their parish; and now, as informal export-import traders, knowing little Spanish and less French, they travel by plane and bring Miami, Port au Prince and Panama into their trading system.

For buyer and seller trading is business and a social occasion. Buying escallion and yams involves swapping news. Goods are for sale but gossip is free. There is a ritual for bargaining. Regular customers look at the goods they have bought and ask 'Where is my mek-up?' The seller laughs and hands over one or two red peppers or a tired tomato. If some vegetables are in short supply, what is scarce is married to what is plentiful; if 'sweet yam', for example, is scarce, it is 'married' to cassava, which is plentiful. Divorce is out of the question, for whom the higgler has joined together let no man put asunder.

Wayside stalls

The wayside stalls are irresistible. Even from a long way off they signal to us to stop. Golden oranges, tangerines of a deep yellow, scarlet ackees threaded on long sticks, large glossy-green avocado pears, papayas (paw-paw) that weigh four or five pounds, yams, sour-sops, whatever is in season – and the owner of each stall composes his own creation-poem out of what he has grown or bought. Nearby a three-year-old sucks an orange. An elder chews a piece of sugar-cane. Two or three hens cluck away in the shade of the nearby cottage. A goat heavy with kid pulls at the grass by the side of the road. A pig and its litter of five root at a clump of bananas. The stall is an extension of the household, tended by grown-ups and by youngsters, a source of ready cash in an economy based in part on subsistence farming.

Often the man or woman tending the stall is ready to talk about the things they grow and the high prices they pay for the fruit and vegetables they buy; and perhaps about the family: seven children, of whom two have grown up and gone away; one is in the police force in Kingston; the other five are still at home, and the two acres of land he owns cannot buy all the clothes and shoes they need. But he is better off than his neighbour Hezekiah Brown who rents the five acres he farms. Hezekiah has been paying rent for twelve years; some months he cannot pay more than the interest. It is better to own, even if it's only a piece of stony hillside. What helps him, he says, is that his wife raises some chickens and keeps a pig. And she is a good cook. When yams are in season they eat yam, and he keeps in reserve a few hills of St Vincent yam because one planting lasts a long time. It spreads itself under the ground, so it is a help in time of need. That is why we call it 'Come-here-fe-help-we' yam. The price of shop-goods has gone up in the sky; high, high; even salt-fish, that was once poor man's food, it has gone high out of reach. It is rich man's food now. Salt-fish gone join up with satellite. And goat mutton gone up there too. A little meat at weekend perhaps, and for the other days, his wife makes some corn-pork stretch a long way.

A smallholder rides out on his donkey to harvest his pimentos

Some well-established holdings are models of an efficient three-tier system of cultivation with tree-cover from breadfruit, ackee and avocado trees. The trees give shade to a small patch of coffee trees and protect the soil. The homes have three or four rooms, and are beautifully kept. But there are too many people on the land, and much of the land is marginal; so the young especially search desperately for a future, in the towns perhaps, or even overseas.

The eldest boy came down the sloping land with us (wrote Peter Abrahams). *He was twenty-one and he'd not been able to find work to help his family. He'd been born here.... Could we help him to get to another country where there was work? Many people had gone abroad looking for work. But he didn't even have a piece of land to sell to go abroad. Perhaps if he could get away he could earn enough to come back and make life better for his family. People go away and come back after some years with enough money to make life better.*

In his book *Jamaica*, Peter Abrahams goes on to tell of a visit to another home on rented land.

[His host] *rented three acres of land but in five separate pieces.... Wouldn't he have preferred to have his land in one parcel? ... You have to take what you can get. He had one pig, one dog and one donkey. He grew yams, bananas, peas, cassava and other food-crops. His average income was $800 a year ... he'd been born here, he'd worked here all his life: and not even a decent house to show for it.... He and his wife had worked hard to give their children a better schooling than they'd had themselves. He wanted the younger ones and his wife to be in a better house than this....*

Lillian Webb brought in the food and wrung my heart by wanting me to share the little they had.

Jamaicans welcome opportunities for seasonal employment in the United States and Canada. An outstanding example of these programmes is the recruitment of West Indians to cut sugar-cane in South Florida. This began in 1943, so the West Indian labour force is now an intrinsic feature of Florida's sugar industry. The most recent study of Caribbean workers in this industry, carried out by the Centre for Latin American Studies

44

of the University of Florida, estimates that in 1980-81 West Indian workers sent back about nineteen million dollars to the sending islands; and it points out that there are three direct beneficiaries of the programme: the participating worker, the worker's home island and the Florida sugar industry.

With limited landspace and most of the exits closed, Jamaicans find themselves in a difficult position. They must keep down their death rate.They are bringing down the birth rate. In order to provide employment for an expanding population they seek access to more markets in North America and they press for more investment in Jamaica from overseas. They are also working to increase the flow of visitors into the island because they wish to attract more foreign exchange and because they value the friendship and understanding of people from other countries.

The government and agriculture

Ever since independence in 1962 the Jamaica Labour Party and the People's National Party have made agricultural reform and improvement priorities, and much has been done. The Government is committed to increasing the agricultural potential of Jamaica by a rural development programme, incentives for producing export crops, strengthening existing commodity organisations for such crops as citrus, coffee and bananas; overhauling the marketing system to get more efficient distribution; providing opportunities for ownership; developing new irrigation programmes; expanding production in the major crops and promoting other crops such as sorghum, maize, castor bean and other oil-seeds and flowers.

One of the most important of the Government-subsidised agencies is the Jamaica Agricultural Society, which acts as a farmers' forum, provides an excellent information service, runs a number of Farmers' Stores that sell seed and supplies, and organises agricultural shows and training courses.

There are island-wide Commodity Associations which supervise the cultivation and manage the marketing of the island's major export crops. During the period 1975-1980 there

45

was a catastrophic fall in the production of many of these crops, and this meant a serious loss of foreign exchange.

The Government of Jamaica has launched a drive to increase sugar and banana production, and it is restructuring the Commodity Associations for these crops as well as for other crops, such as coffee, cocoa and citrus, in order to increase production and exports. Those seeking further information will find these addresses useful:

Agricultural Development Corporation
5 East Street   *and*   46 Trinidad Terrace
Montego Bay   Kingston 5
(tel: 952-2412)   (tel: 926-9160)

Agricultural Information Service
Ministry of Agriculture
Hope Gardens,
Kingston 6
(tel: 927-9831)

Jamaica Agricultural Society
Publicity and Information Service
71 Church Street
Kingston
(tel: 922-0610)

Other resources

The University of the West Indies has a strong Faculty of Agriculture, which is active in research and teaching. It concentrates on studies closely related to the needs of the Commonwealth Caribbean. It is closely associated with the Caribbean Agricultural Research and Development Institute, CARDI, a regional organisation supported by fifteen Caribbean governments.

Some of the bauxite companies that operate in Jamaica have done valuable work in assisting smallholders, improving live-stock management and improving marginal and poor land. Useful addresses are:

University of the West Indies
Public Relations Officer   CARDI
Mona   University of the West Indies
Kingston 7   Kingston 7
(tel: 927-9925)   (tel: 927-6531)

5 The folk –
the cuisine of Jamaica

Jamaicans make poetry in the kitchen. The tradition of flavourful cooking was established by generations of women who started from girlhood and, as grannies, performed miracles on a raised fire-place, with one or two iron pots black from use, one or two bowls of clay called yabbas, and sticks of firewood. There were always one or two in a village who 'cooked sweet', earning the envy of other women and the respect of all the men with their fricasseed chicken, ackee and salt-fish, dip-and-fall-back, rice and peas, and scaveeched fish. They had no clock, no timer but the sun and an inbuilt sensing-device that told them when the stew was ready, or when the wood-fire should be damped down. They had no books of recipes, just their memories, well-developed taste buds and skill in stretching scraps of meat and fish.

These women, whether they worked in the kitchens of the Great House, where meat was plentiful, or as cooks with the growing number of upper and middle class Jamaican families, or in their own kitchens, created the typical dishes of Jamaica. Climate and transplantation to a new environment set limits. Fresh meat and fish had to be used quickly, or salted and cured. Salted cod, mackerel and pickled herring kept better and went further. Pigs, goats and chicken supplied most of the meat that was used, beef being more expensive and not so plentiful. 'Breadkind', the general name for starchy food, was varied, with different kinds of yams (not sweet potatoes, as in parts of the United States), sweet potatoes, bananas, plantains, cassava, eddoes and cocos, along with cornmeal and flour. There was a wide range of vegetables, such as calalu (a Jamaican form of spinach), pumpkin (for soups and as a vegetable but never for pies), cabbages, okra, tomatoes and the like, red kidney beans, locally called red peas, and gungo peas. Here are some typical dishes.

Famous Jamaica dishes

Soups

The basic theory is that soups must have substance. This means thick soups rather than clear; not cream soups but soups thickened with vegetables and 'breadkind', and flavoured with thyme, marjoram and pepper. There are Jamaican versions of such favourites as oxtail soup, fish broth, coco soup, beef soup, and a 'cook-up', a meal in itself that will make a man 'strong as a cow', based on meat, chicken, salt pork and yams and cocos, like the sancocho of Latin American. There are several Jamaican soups that are particularly famous. The first is Jamaica

Bringing in the catch

Pepperpot, a glorious combination of calalu (spinach) chopped fine, okra, soup meat, pigs' tail, onion, garlic and coconut milk with a few shrimps thrown in for good measure. Scotch Bonnet pepper is often found in Jamaica. The Scotch Bonnet pepper is cooked unbroken in the soup so that it adds flavour without heat. Broken, it is lethal. Then there is Red Peas soup, made from the most popular of all the family of peas and beans, the red kidney bean. In Latin America the equivalent is Black Bean soup. Ingredients for this soup should include soup meat and pigs' tail, coco, eddo or yellow yam, escallion, thyme and the unbroken country pepper. Basically the same ingredients are used for Pumpkin soup, which should be made from firm-textured pumpkin of a rich yellow colour. These are soups that lift up a man's soul and make him prophesy.

Seafood

The most highly-prized delicacies are lobster, crab, snapper and king fish. The lobster is in fact a large crayfish, tender and

delicate in flavour. Much rarer nowadays is the black or mountain crab which lives in holes on the land and which in March or April goes down to the sea to lay its eggs. Picking crabs is a tedious business. The meat is flaked, seasoned, mixed with a small quantity of fresh bread crumbs, put back in the shell and baked. No one can bake enough.

Scaveeched fish (pronounced scoveitch) is much the same as the *escabeche* of Latin America. In Jamaica the fish is fried first, then smothered with onion and vinegar and highly spiced with Scotch Bonnet pepper. Very popular also is fried fish. Scaveeched fish and fried fish are eaten with bammies, flat cakes made from cassava flour or meal, half an inch or more in thickness. They are baked or fried and thickly buttered.

Salt-fish, the salted cod from North Atlantic waters, the *bacalao* of Spain and Latin America, is cooked in many ways: as a stew with cho-cho and tomatoes or mixed in with rice, or cooked in with sweet potatoes. Easy to make and very popular are salt-fish fritters, made small in size and very crisp as hors d'oeuvres, or large, with a mixture of flour, for breakfast or lunch. A heavy version of these is stamp-and-go, so named because travellers would stop to buy these fritters at a wayside shop, with a piece of bread, then stamp-and-go. Other fun names are 'poor man fritters' and 'macadam', because they are tough as the asphalted road, and 'John stagger back', from the shock of attempting to bite through them.

The great dish is ackee and salt-fish. Jamaicans argue that a beneficent providence guides us; if it were not so how could the ackee travel from its home in West Africa to meet in Jamaica the salted cod of Newfoundland? Such a marriage must have been made in heaven.

Meat and poultry

The notable dishes are roast pork – the quality of Jamaican pork is excellent – curried goat and fricasseed chicken. East Indians who came to Jamaica in the second half of the last century brought with them their skill in making curry. Jamaican cooks soon became expert at it. Curried goat is a highly spiced peppery dish, but it can be made less inflammable without loss of flavour. The secret of fricasseed chicken is that it should be seasoned with onion, scallion and black pepper overnight. On the following day the pieces of chicken should be wiped dry and browned. Finally, a small quantity of water is added along with tomatoes and a pinch of ginger powder, and then the dish is simmered.

'Breadkind'

Any starchy food is 'breadkind'; ripe plantains can be included. Yam is the great staple. There are many kinds: yellow yam, Lucea yam, sweet yam, renta, St Vincent and yampie. They can all be boiled, or boiled and creamed, or baked in the skin, or crushed and baked with cheese sprinkled on top. In the Jamaican kitchen every visitor should play Columbus, and few discoveries are more delectable than a yampie or sweet yam, fine in texture, baked in the skin, buttered and served steaming hot. Other great favourites are candied sweet potato, baked or roasted breadfruit, green banana boiled and creamed, and fried ripe plantain.

Rice takes its place alongside yam as a favourite, and one of the dishes that all Jamaicans overseas dream of is rice-and-peas, sometimes called Jamaica Coat of Arms. In the Eastern Caribbean this is called peas and rice. The peas used there are pigeon peas, called congo peas; in Jamaica they are called gungu peas. In Latin America the peas are stewed and the rice cooked separately. Jamaica cooks the red kidney bean and rice together. Authentic rice-and-peas requires, first, thick creamy milk from a dry coconut (see page 54), cooked with 1 cup of red kidney beans made tender by soaking and with rice, about three times the quantity of the peas, with some escallion, thyme and black pepper. A very small piece of salt pork is added after the peas have been boiled.

Desserts

If oranges and star-apples are in season, then the natural choice for them is matrimony, a memorable intermingling of orange juice with the edible pulp of the star-apple, a dash of evaporated or sweetened condensed milk, a pinch of nutmeg and some ice. In season for the larger part of the year are guavas, stewed when ripe and served with coconut cream. Baked ripe bananas, also served with coconut cream or heated in a skillet in a mixture of brown sugar and butter, then flambéed with rum, are delicious. Ice cream is often made from the juice of the sour-sop, which has a pleasantly fresh, tart taste of strawberries and apricots. Cold potato pone is served with coconut cream; banana fritters with a dash of fresh lime juice. To start or finish a meal, an extraordinary assortment of fresh fruit is available.

In praise of bammies, patties and spinners

A **bammy** is a flat cake, made from cassava flour or meal. It is round, and from half to one inch thick. Originally this was the cassava bread of the Arawaks and of other mainland Amerindian people. The Africans who were brought to Jamaica learned from the Arawaks how to make 'cassava bread', and they gave to it a name that is not found elsewhere: 'bammy'. In the course of time an indigenous gourmet produced a 'cassava wafer' which can now be purchased in supermarkets.

At first glance a bammy looks, and feels, hard and dry. Soak it for a few hours in milk, then put it in a frying pan with a dab of butter and pan fry it over moderate heat until it is brown on each side. It can also be baked. Five minutes or thereabouts will suffice, depending on the thickness of the bammy. It is a delicious accompaniment to cold meats, soups and stews.

The cassava wafers are more fragile, but not less delicious. Butter the rough side, heat them briefly in an oven or frying pan until golden brown, and serve them at breakfast, or with hors d'oeuvres – or at any time.

PATTIES deserve capital letters. They rate above United States' hamburgers, English pasties, fish and chips or Latin American *tortillas*. They have a highly-spiced, well-seasoned, filling of beef. This is wrapped in a tender yet crisp crust. Jamaicans travel with suitcases and packages of patties; today it is possible to buy patties in Miami, London, Toronto, New York and other cities to which Jamaicans have migrated. They should be eaten hot; altogether they are a satisfying, protein-packed meal.

Spinners are small dumplings, rolled in the hand, about an inch and a half long, not more than half an inch thick at the middle, and tapering at both ends. They are lighter than a full-blooded Jamaica dumpling, which can pull teeth, chewable, firm without being over-demanding, and are an essential ingredient in Jamaican soups. They are perhaps a little like the Italian *gnocchi* but have more substance.

Drinks for every conscience

Drinks are available for every palate and for every conscience. Coconut water is in great demand, especially cool and refreshing from a green nut, which the seller will open with a quick slash of his machete. If you would like to try the jelly he will split the nut open and slice off a tiny portion of the green outside for use as a spoon. Coconut water is good for one; it

A boy climbing a coconut palm

flushes out the kidneys, and is a valuable source of iron; with a dash of lime juice, it helps to lower the blood pressure. Many Jamaicans find it excellent with a dry light rum. Visitors soon learn that the coconut water from the green nuts is not the same as coconut milk, which is obtained from the dry nut by grating the flesh, adding some water and squeezing out the milk.

There are as many varieties of fruit juices and nectars as there are varieties of fruit. Some of the more exotic are the nectars made from guava (an excellent source of vitamin C), mango, sour-sop, paw paw (papaya), tamarind and granadilla. Is there anything more welcome at mid-morning than an ice-cold glass of freshly-squeezed juice from a navel orange?

For rum punch the most commonly used recipe is: One of sour (one part of fresh lime juice); two of sweet (two parts of honey or sugar); three of strong (the rum), and four of weak (water and ice). If it is convenient, frost the glass ahead of time, then mix, shake and take. A drop or two of angostura adds to the flavour.

The local beer, Red Stripe, is excellent, so much so that over the years it has built up a market in Britain, Canada and parts of the United States.

A sample of tested recipes

The most popular and most easily obtained book of Jamaica recipes is *A Merry go round of Recipes from Jamaica*, by Leila Brandon, published and distributed by the Novelty Trading Company of Kingston, Jamaica. It contains recipes for main dishes of meat and fish, soups, desserts, pastry, fruit punches and cocktails. Two other books, which cover the Caribbean, are Slater's *Carribbean Cookery*, and Rita Springer's *West Indian Cookery*.

Wayside eating

Along the coast there are wayside stalls that sell fried fish, with bammy or hard-dough bread. The fish, usually sprat or snapper, is fried with red pepper, escallion, onions and vinegar. With the bammy or bread it makes an excellent meal. If by

Cooking jerk pork

chance the fish is too peppery, the cook may be willing to prepare a milder version; but first try what has been prepared.

Roasted fish may also be available. The fish will probably be turbot or wenchman (from Welchman), or doctor-fish, so-called because it has a sharp movable spine like a doctor's lancet on each side of its tail. Herbs, spices and butter are put inside and around the cleaned fish, which is then wrapped tightly in aluminium foil and put over an open fire. This is well worth stopping and waiting for.

Jerk pork and jerk chicken are popular wayside dishes. The word 'jerk' goes back a long way. In his book *Jamaica Talk*, Cassidy says it is a Spanish word of Indian origin, and it means preparing pork in the manner of the Quichua Indians. The process was taken over by the Maroons, who hunted hogs. Portland is traditionally the parish associated with jerk pork, but it is now widely available. The meat is seasoned with pepper and spices, then grilled slowly over a flat fireplace; the smoke from wood, often guava or pimento, adds to the flavour. If breadfruits are in season, slices of roast breadfruit are a good accompaniment.

There are some interesting drinks available at the stalls, in addition to coconut water or beer. The most popular is Sky Juice, or Earth Juice, a non-carbonated drink made from a syrup with a fruit base, mixed with crushed ice and water and served in a plastic bag with a straw.

Wayside eating places

Wayside eating places have multiplied in recent years. Here are some of the most popular.

Country, near the docks in Port Royal. It sells fish soup, fried fish and bammy. These are also available at stands in the town. Port Royal is a centre for fishing, and the fried fish is good, as is the fish broth or soup, which is esteemed as an aphrodisiac.

Button Bay is just beyond Yallahs, on the road from Kingston to Morant Bay. This is a small fishing centre, so fresh fish is the attraction. Fish and fish soup are available at weekends. Hard-dough bread is the standard accompaniment.

Faith's Pen, four miles east of Moneague on the main road (A3) to Kingston, is one of the gastronomic centres for those who travel by road. A dozen or more stalls offer roasted yam with a sliver of salt-fish roasted in the embers (and high in sodium, alas), boiled corn on the cob (a hard grained variety of yellow corn), ripe bananas and, in season, sweet-sops, sour-sops and avocado pears. Also on sale is soup, the most popular being cow-cod soup, which has been described as being full of bull, which means the procreative parts.

Ocho Rios has jerk pork and chicken and, in season, roasted breadfruit. There is a stall just west of the clock tower in the town. Some stalls can be found alongside the road to the Dunns River Falls, offering fried fish, jerk pork and jerk chicken. There are also stalls at the entrance to the Dunns River Falls. The meat is smoked over logs and branches from the pimento tree, which contain some of the spicy fragrance of the pimento berries.

Runaway Bay has a bar that sells fried fish by the pound.

Negril has its own way with the world and with the English language. A stall in the Plaza proclaims that it has for sale saucy perilla (sarsparilla), chainy root, Irish mash (Irish Moss), lynseed, blood whis, strong back, log wood honey and nutmeg, all served together in one drink. In the same plaza a family-run bakery sells excellent home-baked bread and pastry, as well as some Jamaican dishes, such as ackee and salt-fish baked in a stick of French bread.

Bluefields Beach has roadside stalls that sell fried fish, bammy, shrimps and river crayfish boiled with salt and hot pepper.

Middlequarters is a popular centre for crayfish and fresh water shrimps (which are often pronounced 'srimps' or 'swimps' and which are called 'janga').

From **Porus** to **Clarendon Park** the stalls are gay with fruit, golden oranges and tangerines, yellow grapefruit and ripe bananas, as well as with some ground provisions. In the season packets of freshly roasted cashew nuts are offered for sale.

Most of the wayside stalls offer bread of one kind or another; usually tightly-kneaded, chewy hard-dough bread. Jamaicans delight in bread. Every township in the island has its bakery, each with its own special way of mixing the dough and baking; with its unique way of shaping the loaves, its own special highly-glazed buns and flour-cakes or bullas. The standardised, artificially enriched bread of the world's great urban cities has no charm for a Jamaican. One of the most welcome gifts a Jamaican in exile can receive is an Easter bun or a loaf of hard-dough bread from home.

Cuisine as culture

The cuisine of a country mirrors its culture, its values, history and modes of expression. The Jamaican folk fashioned a cuisine of their own and developed a philosophy about food. Those who know hunger know also that 'Better belly bus' (burst) than good bitle (victual) spoil.' Those who know hardship learn how to share what little they have. They despise those who are mean or 'cubbitch' (covetous). To be greedy or 'craven' is contemptible. To be generous is to join the band of 'deastant' people.

6 The folk –
the springing roots

Where lie the roots?

How can one who wishes to keep company with Jamaica learn about the folklore of the people, the sparkling proverbs, the tales about Anansi the Spider Man, the folksongs, spirituals and the religious cults such as the Rastafarian?

These books will help: *Jamaica Talk*, written by a Jamaican, Fred Cassidy, published by Macmillan of London, which is about the language Jamaicans speak. He is Professor of English at the University of Wisconsin. For more detail consult the *Dictionary of Jamaican English*, by Cassidy and Le Page, published by Cambridge University Press. A number of the folk-tales are re-told in English in *Anansi the Spider Man*, by Philip Sherlock, published by Thomas Y. Crowell, New York. Father Joseph Owens has written about the Rastafarians in *Dread*, published by Sangster-Collins. There is another illuminating study of the movement as a search for identity in Rey Nettleford's *Mirror, Mirror*, published by Sangster. Ivy Baxter's *Arts of an Island* gives an overall account of the performing and creative arts in Jamaica. There are many recordings of reggae and there is an excellent collection of Jamaican Spirituals by Olive Lewin and the Jamaica Folk Singers.

Where lie the roots of Jamaican folk-culture? Are they in the same soil as Canadian or American folk-culture? The United States and Canada have their roots in Europe but, except for American blacks, their cultures were transplanted, not forcibly uprooted. New World blacks, whether in Alabama, Brazil,

Folk dancing at the Plantation Inn

Haiti or Jamaica, faced discontinuity, a break, and the painful process of anchoring roots in a new and often hostile cultural environment. They had no written records. Their stories, history, music, customs and ancestral beliefs were lodged in their minds. Though they were all Africans, they came from many different tribes and regions, spoke different languages, and held different religious beliefs. Some were from the Wolofs and Mandingoes of Senegambia. Others were from the Denkyera, the Fante, Ashanti and Akim people. Yet others were from Dahomey and others were Yorubas, Ibo, Fon and Edo people. They came from a region as large and as diverse as Western Europe. They were brought as individuals, and it was the policy to keep them apart from their compatriots in order to lessen the danger of their combining to foment uprisings.

It would be difficult to find in history a harsher fate than that of the New World blacks, including the African ancestors of the Jamaican people, forcibly uprooted from their homes and countries.

Gradually from their accumulated experience the folk began to put down their roots and to create a new way of life, a culture that was their own. How did they do this? The strongest link between them was not that of tribe or family but of having travelled from Africa on the same slave ship; they were not kinsmen, not fellow tribesmen, but shipmates; it was a relationship of chance, not of blood. They did not know it, but they had little time in which to get acquainted; the life expectation of a slave was seven years. The Arawaks had chosen mass suicide. Some of the Africans chose to die; they pined away. But the majority, without planning, as a natural response to this terrible fate, chose to live, to adjust, to put down their roots. Just as technology is man's response to his environment, so the folk culture of the Jamaican and West Indian folk is a record of a people's response to their new environment. It was a way of meeting their spiritual and psychological needs. The folk, not the governments, not those in authority, established a seed-bed for a national culture; not deliberately, but as part of an agonising process of ensuring that they survived. From this seed-bed has grown a national culture which has ties with other cultures but which is uniquely Jamaican. We can witness this evolution. This is why Jamaica can be a venue for fun and for learning.

Jamaica talk

The late Ken Maxwell wrote a little book that visitors will take to their hearts. It is *How to Speak Jamaican*. Ken described himself as a Jamaican farmer, broadcaster, journalist, clown; as having been born in Vere, lived most of his life in Manchester; as having one wife, a son, a daughter, three horses, two dogs, twenty cows, a twenty-one-year-old car; as having spent his time looking ironically at life and loving what he saw. You will enjoy dipping into his book of forty-five pages and finding that an 'aring' is a citrus fuit known in overdeveloped countries as an orange; that 'Is bare woman in de office' does not mean that all the women in the office are naked, but that there are only women in the office, for 'bare' means 'only'. He reminds us also that 'Come dung out a de tree' means 'come down out of the tree'. Also, of course, cows and horses make 'dung'. Smaller animals make a 'mess'.

Having survived the rigours of *How to Speak Jamaican* why not turn to Cassidy's *Jamaica Talk?* It is a rich treasury of Jamaica's history and of its language; of the inherited language of the folk, fashioned by them as a medium for communicating with each other and with those in control. The chief sources of Jamaica Talk are English and some West African languages, notably the Akan-Ashanti and Ewe language groups. The English were drawn from different parts of England, Scotland, Wales and Ireland, and from different classes. They spoke different forms of English, but theirs was the language of authority and business. Most of the blacks were brought from the coast of West Africa, the two main areas of origin being that of the Akan-Ashanti people, and Dahomey, the home of the Ewe-speaking people. Later, large numbers were brought in from the region of the Bight of Benin, Angola and the Congo. By that time, the Akan and Ewe-speaking slaves were dominant among the Jamaica blacks. This steady flow of Africans reinforced the African influence.

The language that came into being took most of its vocabulary from the dominant group of whites, and much of the pronunciation, intonation, rhythms and grammar from the black majority. What developed was not a language of defeated or depressed people, but of people with a strong sense of the ridiculous, a gift for vivid imagery, for ridicule and irony, for nicknames and epithets, for earthy humour and bawdy cusswords.

I must return for a moment to Ken Maxwell. He dedicated his book to 'all Jamaicans who have found that nowhere else in the world is real English spoken, and to those visitors who would like to take the opportunity to learn to speak properly'. They will soon find that Jamaica Talk is a language of impulse rather than of reflection, of action rather than analysis, denunciation rather than discussion, confrontation rather than compromise, turbulence rather than tranquillity. It presents an instant picture rather than a portrait. My sister's son is Joe but he is known as 'knock knee Joe'. Jasper, who has short legs, is 'duggy-duggy Jasper'. My friend Eric is untidy so he becomes 'bugu yaga Eric'. Names are secondary, and are often treated casually; the identifying mark is some physical characteristic, so we have caricature rather than elaborate characterisation. This is an effective method which conveys an immediate, vivid impression. A precocious girl, for example, is 'force ripe'. A covetous person is a 'big eye man who is never satisfied in dis world'. Repetition and sound convey the meaning. A finicky person is 'fenky-fenky', and one in ragged patched clothes is 'pitchy-patchy'.

The passive voice is rarely used. The tradition is of an oral, not a written language. It expresses the mood of the moment; the speaker uses intonation, repetition, imagery, gesture, filling each word with drama. Lifeless things come to life: I do not drop a cup; the 'wutless something' jump right out of me hand. I do not miss the bus; the bus left me. I do not forget to mail the letter my friend gave me; that letter jus' fly out of me mind. I do not meet a friend; instead I convey the impression of a collision, for 'I buck up with him'.

Irony, satire and ridicule are the dominant characteristics. They are used not only against others but against oneself, to express anxiety, concern or inner doubt. Miss Lou, in her poem celebrating Jamaica's independence in 1962, caught the mood perfectly.

Independence wid a vengeance,
Independence raisin' cain,
Jamaica start grow beard, ah hope
We chin can stan' de strain.

Continuing the mood of pride mingled with self-mockery, how will the new nation fare in a world of super-powers armed with atomic bombs?

We defence is not defenceless
For we got half-a-brick,
We got we broken bottle
And we Cookomacca stick ...

This gift for vivid imagery, so characteristic of West African proverbs, gives Jamaican proverbs the sparkle of sunshine. Instead of the dark sayings of the wise we have the wise sayings

Jamaican artists and musicians

of the dark, each a crystallisation of experience in a single image. Thus, 'hard words break no bones' becomes 'Cuss-cuss (abuse) never bore hole in skin'. Familiarity breeds contempt becomes 'If you play with puppy, puppy lick you mouth'. 'Don't play with edged tools' is vivified as 'You never see dawg chaw razor'.

63

Animals and insects become teachers, warning us against the kind of behaviour that made life difficult for people torn away from a network of tribal and family relationships, powerless against oppression and often short of food. In such circumstances let those in authority remember that when a powerful man falls those who are weak can take advantage of him. 'When cotton-tree fall down even nanny goat jump over him', and 'Every day you goad donkey, one day him will kick you'. The poor dare not show their anger, so 'Poor man never vex'. The powerless should choose their friends with care: 'Not everybody who kin (skins, shows) them teeth wid you is friend'; also, 'Man you can't beat, you have to call him fren''. Be discreet and let the entry of a third person put an end to gossip: 'When six yeye (eyes) meet, story done'. Do not mock at others, remember that 'Little pig ask him mama (mother) what make her mout' so long, she say "Never mind, me pickney, that same thing that make fe me (mine) long will make fe you (yours) long too".' Poor people who show off should remember that 'When dawg mauger (thin) him head big'. Every man needs help, for 'One finger can't catch dog-flea'. Guard the tongue: 'When you go to donkey house don't talk about ears', and look after your own interests, for 'You can't keep crow from flying but you can keep him from pitching on you' head'.

Anansi stories

The chief character in the folktales of Jamaica is Anansi, often spelled Anancy. The word Ananse, a spider, is from the Twi language of West Africa; it also means Creator because he makes something out of nothing, i.e. his web. He symbolises the triumph of wit over brute strength and, like Proteus, he is able to take many forms. The spider's web was often spoken of as 'Anancy rope'. Sometimes, when old women got sleepy, Anansi tied up their faces with his rope.

The Ashanti people brought their spider-god with them across the Atlantic, and with him came his son Tacooma and his wife Crooky. The transplanted people kept alive the West African tradition of story-telling, in which the story-teller dramatised the tale, with Anansi changing from spider to man,

speaking in a high-pitched falsetto and with a lisp. He over-
comes others by guile, and he is the reason why things are as
they are. Why is a dog's belly narrow and squeezed? 'Is Anansi
mek (cause) it.' Why do wasps sting? 'Is Anansi mek it.' And
how did Jackass Head get into John Canoe dance? 'Is Anansi
mek it.'

The stories are delightful, and there are story-tellers who, by
changes of expression and by mimicry are able to transport us
into a magic world where we live through the swift changes of
mood, the cunning and cupidity, the affected anger and actual
greed, the hypocrisy and pretended stupidity, the anxiety and
amusement of Anansi. It is a world of robust, uninhibited
people. Here is a story of Granny Backbone, which illustrates
the narrative style and Anansi's cunning.

*Once upon a time,and a long, long time ago there was a
hard dry-weather time in Anansi country; a dry, dry time
and only one man have water. No rain, river dry up,
stream dry up, and only one man have water. The man
name was Ho-Ho-Hee-Hee, and he have a well that never
dry up. Only Ho-Ho-Hee-Hee have water, but you can
only get the water if you guess the man name; for that
man never use him real name, never, never. He go by the
name Granny Backbone, and him wife name was Mrs
Granny Backbone.*

*Now Anansi have no water. Crooky have no water.
There is no water in the house. The little stream down by
the banana tree dry up. So Anansi say to Crooky: 'There
is one man have water. We must go and get water from
him. We mus' go to Granny Backbone and get water from
him. If we don't get the water we going dead like the
banana tree dead. We will dry up like the little spring dry
up.'*

*So Crooky say, 'But Anansi, you can't get the water
from Granny Backbone because you don't know him
name. If you don't know him real name you can't get the
water.'*

*'I have a plan to find out the name, Crooky. I have a
plan, a good plan that can't fail. You dress me up like a
baby. I will mek myself look small, small like baby. Dress
me up like baby, and beg Mrs Granny Backbone to look*

*after me till you come back.' So Anansi mek himself small
and Crooky dress him up like baby, and go round to Mrs
Granny Backbone house. Now Mrs Granny Backbone have
a weak back an' she like to sit down. So Crooky go round
to Mrs Granny Backbone and she find her sitting down in
front of the house. And she put on sweet mouth and say:
'What a pretty, pretty place, Mrs Granny Backbone. A
pretty, pretty house you have.' Mrs Granny Backbone like
to hear that word and she say, 'Crooky, I will show you,
because the yard and the house is really pretty, pretty so
till.' Then, as they go round and Crooky admire
everything she say: 'Oh Mrs Granny Backbone, I have to
go down to the shop. I beg you to look after the baby for
me till I come back.'*

*Now Mrs Granny Backbone love to sit down and rock
in her rocking chair and she like to nurse baby, so she sit
down in the rocking chair and she say, 'Give me the baby.
I will look after him till you come back.' She tek the baby
and say 'Oh what a pretty, pretty baby. But him terrible
big and strong, strong for true.' So she sit down and rock,
and Crooky leave her and go down the road, and she rock
and rock and she rub her han' over the baby belly and she
sing for him. And she rock and rock and laugh to herself
an' say 'People so foolish. They can't get water till they
find out me husband real name. But them so stupid they
will never find out.' And she laugh and pat the baby and
stroke the baby belly and she say 'Is a name them will
never know. How them to find out that the name is Ho-
Ho-Hee-Hee. Them will never find out.' She laugh and she
rub the baby belly and the baby leg, and laugh and laugh
at how people so stupid. Then of a sudden she stop laugh.
She get serious of a sudden. She never believe what her
hand tell her. Her eye get wide, and big, and her bottom
lip fall. 'What kind of baby this? What happen? What
happen?' She lift the baby clothes. She take a peep. 'Lord,'
she bawl out, 'Lord have mercy, when Baby ever stay like
dis, when baby ever big like this?' She so frighten she fall
out of the rocking chair and kick and kick an' bawl out 'I
never see baby like dat,' and she never stop bawl out an'
kick till she see her husband come.*

The same time that Mr Granny Backbone come, Crooky
come back for the baby. She tell Mr Granny Backbone she
like the house an' she like the yard and how it pretty,
pretty, and how Mrs Granny Backbone is such a kind lady
to look after her baby, but the time come now to take the
baby back. As she bend down an' take up the baby from
out of the rocking chair where Mrs Granny Backbone did
leave it Anansi put him mouth near her ears and him say
the name. And Crooky turn to Mr Granny Backbone and
say 'I give thanks, I give thanks for true because you and
your wife good to me and look after the baby. And here is
me calabash, I come for water, and I bring this calabash
because it can hold plenty water. So, thank you, Mr Ho-
Ho-Hee-Hee, come fill up me calabash with water quick,
for I thirsty, thirsty fit to die.' Granny Backbone so
frighten when he hear the name that he fall down and beat
him head on the hard ground and Crooky and Anansi go
to the spring and fill up the calabash, and as them go
through the gate them call out loud 'Tanks for the water,
Mr Ho-Ho-Hee-Hee.'

Folk-songs and spirituals

One of the best known of the folk-songs tells of a woman at
Linstead market at evening time, the mangoes in her basket
unsold, her children hungry at home. Those who passed by
took up the mangoes, felt them to see if they were ripe, and
went away without buying even a quattie (3 cents) worth. The
woman sings sadly:
'Carry me ackee go a Linstead market,
Not a quattie worth sell,
Carry me ackee go a Linstead market,
Not a quattie worth sell,
Lord, what a night, not a bite,
What a Saturday night,
Everybody come feel-up feel-up
Not a quattie worth sell . . .'
Perhaps the loveliest of these songs is 'Day dah light' (the day
is dawning). It was sung by women who had been working on

the wharf all night, loading a waiting ship with bananas, each carrying a heavy bunch on her head at the double, then hurrying back for another bunch; at last daybreak comes and the run slows to a walk. They call out to the tally-man who has kept count of the bananas they carried and the money they earned, and sing:

'Day oh, day oh,
Day dah light an' me wan' fe go home,
Day oh, day oh,
Day dah light an' me wan' fe go home,
Come Mr Tallyman, come tally me banana,
Day dah light an' me wan' fe go home.'

Some songs ridicule failings and follies, as in the picture of a man who, years ago, went off to Colon to work on the Panama Canal. He made money and came back with a fine suit, complete with waistcoat and a watch, the chain of which he wore in the fashionable way, across his stomach. But he was not able to read. He still told the time by the sun:

'One, two, three, four, Colon man dah come,
One, two, three, four, Colon man dah come,
Brass chain dah lick him belly bam, bam bam,
You ask him for the time
Him look upon de sun . . .'

Much more shattering is the mockery of a woman abandoned by her soldier lover while she is expecting their child:

'What's de use of you shawl-up, shawl-up
Gal, you character gone,
What's de use of you lace-up, stays-up
What's de use of you lace-up, stays-up
Gal, you character gone . . .'

Jamaican folk-songs and spirituals reveal how Jamaicans see the world and see themselves. A Jamaican poetess and actress, Louise Bennett Coverley, loved by Jamaicans as Miss Lou, has given permanence to the moods and vision of the folk in her poems, published under the title *Jamaica Labrish*. She has been described as the only poet who has really hit the truth about the society through its own language.

In her poem 'Back to Africa', the aspirations of the Back to Africa movement are seen as a defiance of common sense. As Rex Nettleford points out, 'migrating in search of a job makes sense but migrating in search of roots is hardly sensible since Jamaica is home, for that is where you are, "ah right deh (there) you deh (you are)".'

'Back to Africa Miss Matty
You nuh know what you dah say,
You have fe come from someweh (somewhere) fus
Before you go back deh ...
Accorden to dat, all dem blue-y'eye (blue eyes)
White American
Who-fa (Whose) great grandpa was American
Mus' go back a England ...
Go a foreign, seek you fortune,
But no tell nobody say
You dah go seek you homelan
For ah right deh (its right there) so you deh (that you are).'

There were other pioneers, but it is Miss Lou who has fed the power and vision of the folk-songs into the mainstream of Jamaica's culture.

The Jamaica spirituals and revivalist songs have a haunting beauty. Olive Lewin, Founder and Director of the Jamaica Folk Singers, a distinguished group of Jamaican singers, has pioneered the collection and presentation of these songs. In her collection there is a moving song about a gathering in heaven.

'Who will go and die for Adam, ...
When the question was asked in heaven
There was half an hour silence
There was half an hour silence
Who will go and die for Adam?
    I will go,
    I will go.'

There is a lovely song about Mary:
'Although the road be rocky and steep
I ask my Saviour to be my guide,
And when I turn my eyes up to heaven
I saw Mary at her Master feet ...'

Jamaicans are deeply religious in more than a church-going sense. There are the services on Sunday and there are cults and 'revivalists', people who seek 'to live right'; memorial dances to put the dead at rest; white-robed sisters bending and swaying to the hypnotic rhythm of hand-clapping and the tapping of feet; a

69

belief in a spirit world and in life after death. The spirit world is not remote or separate from the world of the living, but forms a unity with it.

The Rastafarians

The Ras Tafari movement began to take shape in the 1930's, a decade in which social discontent erupted in a series of volcanic explosions throughout the archipelago, from Cuba to Trinidad and beyond to Guyana. The causes were widespread unemployment, frustration at being doomed to squalor and anger at being rejected by those in power in the society and by those who were better off and better educated. The anger was intensified by Mussolini's attack on Ethiopia, another example of white oppression of blacks.

Groups of Rastafarians emerged in the slums of West Kingston. Having been rejected by the white world, they in their turn rejected all forms of white power and rule, including the Christian Church. Jamaica was Babylon, Hell, and there was no hope for it. They echoed Marcus Garvey's demand for a return to the homeland, Africa. They based their teaching on the Old Testament and the Book of Revelation. They worshipped a black God, Haile Selassie, Emperor of Ethiopia. They believed that they were the re-incarnation of the ancient Israelites, and that they had been exiled to the West Indies for their transgressions. They believed also that, just as the scattered tribes of Israel had been redeemed and brought back from Babylon, so they would be redeemed and taken back to Africa. They were sons of the mighty God Jah. Each son of Jah has direct contact with the Father. No son of Jah dies. At the heart of their religious system is the notion of their divinity and 'the first-person image of self'. Those who had been rejected, who had been outcasts in the society, became in their eyes, the centre of the Cosmos. There are variations of style and differences of doctrine. Some Rastas wear dreadlocks, following the prohibition in the Book of Leviticus against shaving the hair. Others are bald-headed. Some are poor, from the masses. Others are from middle-class homes, frustrated young people who reject the traditional West Indian values and the existing social structure. Whether the doctrines are true or false, and however bizarre they might seem, Rastafarianism gave to the Brethren a sense of identity, of personal worth, of purpose, of a future.

This affirmation of identity expresses itself in a refusal to use the personal pronoun 'me' which is regarded as a mark of subservience, of acceptance of the role of being an 'object'. A Rastafarian uses the pronoun 'I', the plural of which is 'I-and-I' or 'I-n-I'. The reflexive is 'I-self' or 'I-n-I self'. Using this form, the words of Jesus, 'I testify on my own behalf and the Father who sent me . . .' becomes 'I testify on I own behalf and the Father who sent I . . .'

Ganga, *Cannabis sativa,* is a sacred herb for all Rastafarians. They speak of it as 'wisdom weed' or the 'holy weed'. 'The chalice' or 'cup' is the pipe used for smoking the weed. They testify also to its healing power. You can drink it as a tea, or rub your skin with the ashes, or smoke it; and the Lord God is a smoker, for in the book of Genesis we read that 'God says, Behold, I have given you every herb bearing seed, which is upon the face of the earth' . . . and Psalm 18 tells how 'There went up a smoke out of his (The Lord's) nostrils, and fire out of his mouth devoured; the coals were kindled by it.'

Rastafarians defend their use of ganga by insisting on the 'weed's' sacred character, and by attacking the double standards that prevail in Babylon, which permits the use of alcohol and tobacco. The use of ganga is the central point of conflict between the Rastas and the Government of Jamaica.

The movement has changed greatly since the early days of police harassment and public contempt. There are now rich Rastas as well as poor; influential and internationally known Rastas as well as obscure Brethren. These changes will raise problems for the followers of Ras Tafari. There is no doubt, however, that the discovery of identity and personal worth has profoundly influenced the cultural and social development of Jamaica. A great flood of creative energy has been released. Painters are producing work of great beauty and power. So are the sculptors. Names to bear in mind are Dunkley, Everald Brown, Kapo. These are among the leading 'intuitives', a term applied by David Boxer, Director of the National Gallery, and other Jamaican critics, to those artists whose vision is pure and

A Jamaican craftsman at work

sincere. 'They are for the most part self-taught. Their visions (and many are true visionaries) as released through paint or wood, are unmediated expressions of their individual relationships with the world around them, and the world within.' Boxer, in a catalogue of the first exhibition of Jamaican Intuitive art, emphasised that 'a stream emerges, a school if you will, that rivals, and for me outshines the other great Caribbean outpouring of "primitive art", the Haitian school.'

Music also became a medium through which Bob Marley, the Reggae band, Third World, Burning Spear, Peter Tosh, Jimmy Cliff, Dennis Brown and others have voiced a message against injustice, and have given comfort to the oppressed. As Bob Marley sang:

Fly away home to Zion, fly away home,
One bright morning when my work is over
I will fly away home . . .

The Dance, the Yard Theatres and the small theatres are vibrant examples of this new Jamaica which has its roots in the people's past and which manifests their creativity.

The Government of Jamaica supports this cultural flowering through a well-organised group of institutions, including the Jamaica Festival Commission, the Institute of Jamaica, the Jamaica School of Music, the Jamaica National Trust Commission, the National Council on Libraries, Archives and Documentation, The Jamaica Central Library, the Jamaica School of Art, the Jamaica School of Dance, the Jamaica School of Drama and the Junior Centres. Within the School of Music there is a small but active Folk Music Research Unit under the direction of Olive Lewin. The Institute of Jamaica publishes the *Jamaica Journal* twice a year as well as a number of books on various aspects of the island's history and culture.

7 The long road to independence

Independent Jamaica

On 6 August, 1962 Jamaica became an independent nation. On that day the Parliament of Jamaica met to receive from HRH Princess Margaret, representing the Queen, the documents that established Jamaica's constitutional standing. The first Prime Minister of the independent country, Alexander Bustamante, received the documents and the leader of the Opposition, Norman Washington Manley, joined in the ceremony, making a three-minute speech that is still remembered as one of the finest he ever made. He affirmed what independence means to Jamaicans everywhere.

> We here today stand surrounded by an unseen host of witnesses, the men who in the past and through all our history strove to keep alight the torch of freedom in this country. No one will name them today but this House is in very deed their memorial . . .
>
> And what of the future that lies before us? We have come to independence prepared and ready to shoulder our new responsibilities and united I believe in one single hope that we may make our small country a safe and happy place for all our people . . .
>
> Many of us dare to believe that this country, so blended in origins, so fashioned in time, so wrought on by our own history may go out into the world to make a contribution larger than our size would lead one to expect.
>
> I believe that as an independent nation we can so

*manage ourselves as to demonstrate how by making our
great motto 'Out of many one people 'come to speak the
truth about ourselves, we can become a worthwhile and
shining example of the sort of world men sometimes dream
to live in.*

*You, Princess, have handed us the formal title deeds to
our heritage. For us the task is to plough the land and
gather the fruit.*

Growth of a democracy

The Parliament which assembled on 6 August, 1962 grew
gradually over a period of eighteen years, each stage in its
growth being a result of pressure from the people and their
elected representatives.

The first step was taken in 1944, when the British
Government acceded to a demand that adult suffrage should be
introduced. The demand was not new. It had been made in the
English-speaking countries of the Caribbean from time to time,
but the social upheavals of the 1930's added urgency to the
demand. The 1830's had been a decade of emancipation and of
the emergence of a peasantry, which wanted 'land of my own'
and 'did not care to hire themselves out again'. The 1930's was a
decade of liberation and of insistence on the right 'to govern my
own country' and 'to stand on our own feet'. The introduction
of adult suffrage took place first in Jamaica; but within a few
years it was introduced in most of the countries of the
Commonwealth Caribbean.

Slowly, by a series of constitutional reforms, the power to
govern Jamaica was transferred from the Crown to the country's Parliament. Full internal self-government was achieved in
1957. The final step was taken in 1962, with the granting of
independence.

These changes, and their nature, were determined by leaders
who emerged from among the people of Jamaica; but they were
made possible by the response of the mass of the people. Let us
look, now, at some of these leaders.

An Independence Day Parade in Kingston

Alexander Bustamante

Norman Manley

Marcus Garvey

Alexander Bustamante

Alexander Bustamante was born in 1884 of a lower middle-class family of very limited means. He was an extrovert with a remarkable zest for life and a delight in people. He left Jamaica when he was twenty, travelled widely in Cuba, Panama, the United States and Spain, came back to Jamaica at the age of fifty, and soon attracted attention by his championship of the masses and his attacks on the privileged and powerful. He founded the Bustamante Trade Union, became the acknowledged labour leader of Jamaica, was charged with sedition and thrown into detention camp in 1942. He was released later in 1942, founded the Jamaica Labour Party, swept to power in the elections of 1944, and thereafter for thirty years dominated Jamaican politics.

'Busta' was the kind of man around whom legends gather. He was six feet two inches in height, bony and angular in the style of Abraham Lincoln with a great shock of hair and long arms that appeared to be telescopic; when he was gesturing with them in front of a crowd they seemed to grow longer and longer.

We can form an impression of 'Busta' or 'The Chief' as a person by looking at him through the eyes of a cub reporter of the time, Ulric Simmonds, and of Hugh Foot, formerly Governor of Jamaica, now Lord Caradon.

I remember how good he was with crowds [Ulric Simmonds wrote]. *'How he could move them, sway them and keep them tightly under control or move them to violent action at other times . . . but no one would touch me because I was with Busta.* [Lord Caradon wrote] *He sometimes appears reckless and irresponsible, or rather he used to in his earlier days, but always he shrewdly calculates the effect of his action . . . we soon discovered when he became Minister that he had an astonishingly quick and sure grasp of administrative problems and a political sense which was almost uncanny.*

A man of great charisma, Busta knew intuitively how to maintain his leadership. He was the dynamite that broke up the traditional barriers of privilege and colour in Jamaica. He saw people and not colour or rank. Light-brown himself, he identified with and was accepted by the predominantly black masses. He shattered the colour bar that had separated Jamaicans for centuries.

Norman Manley

Norman Manley was born in 1894 of a lower middle-class family. He spent his early years on a derelict property which his widowed mother managed.

> The property, [he said,] carried on as best it could with a little of everything, logwood, a few cattle, a few tenants, a little cocoa. She made all our clothes, made jellies when guavas were in, kept a small chicken farm and ran things with firm efficiency. When night came she disappeared into her own room to write letters to her few remaining friends, nearly all of whom deserted her when she married a near-black man . . .

Manley won a Rhodes scholarship, entered Oxford to study law and read for the bar, but enlisted in an artillery regiment in World War I with his brother, Roy, who had been denied a commission because he was not white. Roy was killed in action. Norman was awarded the Military Medal for bravery. He returned to Oxford after the war, was Prizeman at Gray's Inn and took first-class Honours in his Bar finals. He married his cousin Edna Swithenbank who in time became Jamaica's most distinguished sculptor, returned to Jamaica, and soon became the island's foremost lawyer. He became leader of the emerging national movement and formed the People's National Party in 1938.

Manley was an introvert who reached his conclusions by analysis. He recognised Jamaica's need for a vital sustaining principle, 'a spirit of national unity', and for institutions which expressed and sustained that spirit. His single most important contribution was ensuring that the 1944 constitution granted the right to vote to all adult Jamaicans. Bustamante swept the Jamaican working class into the mainstream of Jamaican political life and Norman Manley secured the constitutional changes that put political power in their hands.

Although cousins, the two men were very different; extrovert and introvert, intuitive and analytic, mass orator and advocate, they complemented each other. They were opponents but never enemies, adversaries but always Jamaicans. Around them Jamaica's two chief trade unions and political parties took shape and grew. Their example of respect for democracy, for Parliament and the Constitution kept the young nation stable and engendered in Jamaicans of all classes pride and confidence in their country. They did not generate the spirit of independence. That manifested itself at the very start of the settlement of Jamaica, with the Maroons and the slave risings; through the rise of a black peasantry and the dynamism that sent thousands of Jamaicans overseas in search of larger opportunities; through the mass acceptance of Garvey; and through working class struggles and a sophisticated understanding of the political process and of political issues. Independent Jamaica grew out of the spirit of independence of the Jamaican people.

The forerunners – JAGS and Garvey

Two men prepared the Jamaican people for the changes that came in the 1940's. Without them neither Manley nor Bustamante could have achieved all that they did. One was JAG Smith, a black man who by hard work and determination qualified as a barrister (which meant eating his 'dinners' at one of the English Inns of Court) and for a long period was an elected member of the Jamaica Legislative Council. In a period when British officials were regarded as sacrosanct, JAGS made it his special task to reduce the official to his proper status in the country. 'No flattery,' said Norman Manley, 'no offer of any sort of honour or praise would deflect him from his single-mindedness; to teach officialdom that in this country the people's legislature was superior from the Jamaican point of view.'

The other leader was Marcus Garvey. JAGS was on the national stage, Garvey on the international. He was born in St Anns Bay in 1887, travelled as a young man in Central America and was greatly disturbed at the injustices and indignities suffered by blacks. Later, on a visit to England, he had his eyes opened to his mission by Booker T Washington's *Up From*

Slavery; he wrote, '... my doom ... of being a race leader dawned upon me.' Garvey's story is part of world history because, on a vast scale, he led blacks to free themselves from a deep-rooted feeling of inferiority and facelessness in a white world. Though he was rejected by the upper and middle classes of his own country, he contributed to the growth of a national spirit in Jamaica by attacking the false standards of racial values and by pioneering the development of an island-wide political party organisation. His American experience taught him the value of organised political activity and of clearly-stated party programmes; practically every objective he set for his People's Political Party of 1929 was taken over and achieved by the parties of the two political leaders who followed him.

We have been looking at the near-past, the last fifty years of Jamaica's history and the men who shaped it. To understand Jamaicans we need to go farther back in time, for these men were themselves the children of protest; and that protest started in the first years of our history. Moreover, it started among the folk, the enslaved blacks.

Step back in time

Our history, as Jamaicans, begins abruptly, with the English conquest of the island in 1655. By then the first Jamaicans, the Arawaks, had been wiped out. It is more correct to think of them as the first dwellers in Jamaica who had a sense of the region, being blood relations of the Arawaks in the other islands of the Caribbean. The Spanish colonists were driven out in the years between 1655 and 1660. Their fugitive slaves, the Maroons, remained in the hill country. Indigenous Jamaica began with them.

The decisive periods are easily defined. First, Jamaica was a pirates' nest, a buccaneers' base. This was the period of Henry Morgan and of Port Royal. When we visit Port Royal we relive those days. They belong to British imperial, rather than to Jamaican, history.

More decisive, though less spectacular, was the arrival of Henry Modyford, a Barbadian sugar planter, who came to Jamaica as governor in 1664. He brought with him seven

Fort Charles, Port Royal

hundred Barbadian farmers. Barbados was the first place in the Caribbean where the sugar industry was established. The Spanish settlers in Cuba and Jamaica had planted sugar-cane and had processed sugar, but not on the scale that was developed later in north-east Brazil, where the industry was based on the mass production of one crop by the exploitation of large tracts of land and large numbers of slaves. Morgan died in 1688. An earthquake destroyed Port Royal in 1692. By 1700 Jamaica was moving into the age of sugar. No one could have guessed that in a few years the estates would be yielding profits greater than all the booty Morgan ever won.

Sugar islands

Sugar was to the 17th and 18th centuries what oil is to our century. Like a powerful magnet it brought traders crowding into the Caribbean each year from the ports of Western Europe and North America. Sugar set the fleets and armies of Europe grappling with each other. Sugar made the plantation islands more valuable parts of the British empire than was New England. It induced France to yield the whole continent of North America east of the Mississippi to Britain for the return of Guadeloupe and Martinique. It produced the wealth that dazzled Britain. It produced the money that financed the industrial revolution in Britain and in France, and it enabled the West Indian interest to control so many seats in the House of Commons and to gain so much political power that Benjamin Franklin confessed they far outweighed the Northern colonies.

That was one side of the story. The wealth flowed from large plantations manned by black labour. In the course of three hundred and fifty years sugar brought more than ten million blacks from West Africa to the New World. Throughout the islands and in north-east Brazil the unit of production was the same, the sugar and slave plantation.

The growth of the industry was much more than the spread of a profitable crop. It changed the racial composition and social structure of the islands. It resulted in the spread of large estates wherever sugar could be grown, with ownership in the hands of a small number of white owners, many of whom lived in England; in the importation of large numbers of Africans, so that by the end of the 18th century blacks in Jamaica outnumbered whites by ten to one. It meant also a regime of exploitation of both labourer and land, and it was supported by a system of discrimination based on skin colour.

Two Jamaicas

Two Jamaicas came into existence, with two sets of people who lived in the same island, were engaged in producing one crop, but who lived in worlds that were very different. The layout of the plantations mirrored the differences, with Great House and slave huts, fields of sugar-cane on the fertile lowlands and the provision grounds of the blacks on marginal land. Both societies were profoundly affected by the moulding forces. Colonialism bred habits of dependence and of reliance on some external authority. The system of slavery engendered attitudes of superiority among whites and of inferiority among blacks. The plantation system, as it was managed, led to the destruction of natural resources. Because the economic and social system was restrictive, it created counter-movements, the 'haves' resisting change, and the 'have-nots' struggling for change.

Black protest took many forms: sabotage and 'go-slows' on the plantations, malingering and the like; running away, mutinies and rebellion. In Jamaica no African name sounded more clearly than those of Ashanti and Coromanti. 'These,' reported a West Indian planter, 'were accustomed to war from infancy, were energetic of mind, hardy and robust, but bringing with them into slavery lofty ideas of independence, they are dangerous inmates of a West Indian plantation.' Codrington, Governor of the Leeward Islands, spoke of them as not only the best and most faithful of our slaves, 'but [they] are really all born heroes. There never was a rascal or coward of that region.' The will for change, the capacity for leadership and the dynamism were rooted in the mass of the people.

Rise of a peasantry

The next climatic event was the emancipation of all slaves in the

British Empire, in 1832. The slave was no longer another man's property. He was free to sell his labour to the estate or to withold it. Ten years later, the British Parliament established free trade and removed the preferential tariff on West Indian sugar. Emancipation and free trade destroyed the old slave-and-sugar plantation. The Jamaican people set about building homes and free villages often with the help and guidance of Baptist and Methodist missionaries. William Knibb, who had fiercely opposed slavery and had championed the cause of emancipation, wrote: 'By the census taken during last year I find that there were full 19 000 persons, formerly slaves, who had purchased land on which they were erecting their own cottages.' Most countries start with a peasantry. Jamaica started late, but in the years between 1834 and 1850 a black peasantry emerged.

The old representative system remained. It was in fact an oligarchy, political power resting in the hands of a small group of planters and merchants. In 1865, following a rising of black peasants in Morant Bay, the House of Assembly surrendered its powers and Jamaica was ruled by a governor who represented the British sovereign. The small class which had ruled Jamaica since 1660, when the system of representative government was introduced, lost much of its power. It retained considerable influence, however, and, since the franchise for elections to the Legislative Council was restricted, it kept its place as part of the political system. The great mass of the people were excluded. The two Jamaicas remained, divided by colour and ethnic origin. The old plantation system had been destroyed but the attitudes it had engendered still divided the society. The power of the plantocracy had been greatly diminished but the élite jealously guarded its preserves. On the other hand colonialism had been strengthened, and the society remained essentially conservative. The social structure remained that of a pyramid, with a small élite of white and brown at the top, a larger middle layer of brown and a few black middle-class people, and a large base of black peasants.

The dynamism was in the base. By 1860, less than thirty years after emancipation, Jamaica had more than 50 000 holdings of under fifty acres each. By 1900 the number had risen to 130 000. The number of holdings in the five to fifty acre range increased. There was a shift from provision grounds to mixed farming, combining ground provisions for the domestic market with export crops such as ginger, bananas, coconuts and logwood. In 1850 the produce of the Jamaican peasantry was about eighty-three per cent ground provisions and about eleven per cent export crops. In 1890 the percentage of export crops was twenty-three. Reviewing this record, a Royal Commission which visited Jamaica in 1897 pointed out that the peasantry were a source of economic and political strength.

By 1920 there were several critical issues for Jamaica. Could racial discrimination be brought to an end? Could Jamaica produce leaders who would build a spirit of national unity? Could these leaders bring all Jamaicans into the political system and put their future in their own hands?

These were the questions that Garvey, JAG Smith, Bustamante and Norman Manley raised and answered. This is why this brief account started with their names.

The system of government

Like many other independent countries which were formerly part of the British Empire, Jamaica chose to remain a member of the British Commonwealth, the head of which is the British Sovereign. The Governor-General of Jamaica represents the Sovereign. He is named by the Prime Minister of Jamaica, and then appointed by the Sovereign. The Governor-General has no power but that of veto, and this can only be exercised on the advice of the Cabinet.

Power rests with the party elected to govern the country, normally for a period of five years. All Jamaicans over eighteen years of age have the right to vote. The leader of the party that wins the election is invited by the Governor-General to be Prime Minister and to form a government. The Prime Minister appoints the Ministers of Government. These form the Cabinet, which formulates government policy and proposes it to the House of Representatives.

The legislature consists of two houses, the House of Representatives and the Senate. Members of the House of Representatives are elected, each member representing one of the constituencies into which the island is divided. The House appoints from amongst its members a Chairman, the Speaker, who presides over the meetings of the House and sees that parliamentary procedure is observed.

The Senate is a nominated body. Members are appointed by the Governor-General on the advice of the Prime Minister. The leader of the opposition names a stated number of those to be appointed. The chief function of the Senate is to review legislation sent forward by the elected House.

Law and administration

To safeguard its independence and impartiality the Judiciary is separate from the Legislature. The Chief Justice, Judges of the Supreme Court and of High Courts, judges, magistrates, Justices of the Peace and members of the police force are Jamaicans.

Security is in the hands of the Jamaica police force and the Jamaica Regiment, which consists of men recruited in Jamaica and under the command of Jamaican officers.

Local government is administered by two bodies: elected Councillors of a number of cities or municipalities, each Council having the right to elect a Mayor; and elected members of Parish Councils. Each Parish Council receives grants from the Central Government to assist it in carrying out its business.

The Civil Service administers the business of central Government. In each Ministry there is a Permanent Secretary, a career official who advises the Minister but does not make policy. He is responsible for carrying out decisions taken by the government. The Civil Service has two main branches, the technical and administrative, and the clerical.

Civil servants have permanent full-time appointments. They do not lose their jobs when a new government is elected to power. All matters affecting the service, such as promotions, complaints and training, are dealt with by an independent body, the Jamaica Public Service Commission.

In addition to the departments in each Ministry there are a number of Boards or Commissions which are set up to perform certain specific duties. These are known as Statutory Boards. They include the Jamaica Broadcasting Commission, the

Jamaica Industrial Development Commission, the Agricultural Development Corporation, the Yallahs Valley Authority and the Jamaica Tourist Board.

2 A Visitor's Guide

How Part Two is organised

Now it is time, as we say in the island, for my foot to take the road: but to what destination? And in search of what attractions?

Part Two sets out the options. The text gives

(a) a brief description of the location;
(b) basic information;
(c) a list of hotels, guest houses, villas (with capsule descriptions);
(d) a list of restaurants and cafes;
(e) things to do and see;
(f) tours.

8 Planning and getting ready

Sources of information

Good planning saves travellers money and time, and makes a vacation a worthwhile investment. Good planning, however, calls for a base of reliable up-to-date information. One of the best sources for information about travel and accommodation in Jamaica is the Jamaica Tourist Board, a government agency charged with responsibility for developing tourism in Jamaica and providing information to intending visitors as well as to those already in the island.

The Board publishes lists of hotels, guest houses and resort catalogues. It produces attractive brochures about Jamaica and its resort centres, and can also give up-to-date information about a wide range of activities, entertainment and investment opportunities.

The head office of the Board is in the Sheraton complex in New Kingston, Knutsford Boulevard, Kingston 5, Jamaica, (tel: (809) 929-8070). The Board has branch offices at Montego Bay, Negril, Ocho Rios and Port Antonio. The addresses of these branch offices and the telephone numbers are given at the end of this chapter.

There are offices of the Jamaica Tourist Board in Miami, New York, Chicago, Toronto and London. The addresses of these offices are also given at the end of this chapter. Enquiries will be dealt with promptly and efficiently. In addition to asking the Board for information about travel and hotels, request also copies of brochures such as 'Your Vacation Guide to Jamaica' which is published by Creative Communications Ltd, PO Box 105, Kingston 10 (tel; 929-2273). Ask also for contacts through

Some of the beach hotels at Ocho Rios

the Board's imaginative Meet-The-People Programme and request information about the Jamaica Attractions Development Company (JADCO). If you list your special interests, whether it be reggae, discos, scuba diving, hiking and camping, exploring caves, games and water sports, bridge, bird watching or whatever, the Board will be able to advise you about contacts and facilities.

Two other useful addresses for those interested in hotel accommodation, or in renting apartments or villas, are the Jamaica Hotel and Tourist Association, 2 Ardenne Road, Kingston 10 (tel: 926-3635) and the Jamaica Association of Villas and Apartments (JAVA) at the same Ardenne Road address, (tel: 927-0405). This Association is listed under JAVA in the Jamaica Telephone Directory. It has a branch office in Ocho Rios (tel: 974-2508).

The next step is to select a travel agent who is within easy reach and has a good reputation. Even travellers allergic to travel agents are finding that in these days of mass travel and multiple choice the business of working out convenient connections and finding the most reasonably priced routes has become too complicated for the amateur. Anyone having difficulty in finding a suitable agent should seek the assistance of either the American Society of Travel Agents, 360 Lexington Avenue, New York, or of the Association of British Travel Agents, 50-57 Newman Street, London W1P 4AH. Generally, carriers and tour operators pay the travel agent a fixed commission, so his services for reserving transportation and for writing up the ticket should cost the client nothing. He can also assist with working out the itinerary and making all reservations at a fee of between ten and fifteen per cent. Tour operators are committed to promoting their own special lines so a well-established independent travel agent, who serves as expert and counsellor, is the best guide through the confused turmoil of today's international travel bazaar.

Travel styles and travel options

The styles of travel depend on personal taste, cost and convenience. The options include all-inclusive group tours, or travelling as an individual (FIT) with arrangements paid for in advance, or travelling with a minimum of pre-arranged features. Each style carries its plus and its minus. Group tours provide a feeling of security, freedom from having to adjust to another culture, from anxiety about changes in the standard of accommodation and about the possibility of an unfriendly reception. They offer a range of contacts with fellow-citizens whom one would never have met in any other way. All these are available within a known budget and known time-table. In return for these advantages the traveller accepts certain constraints: arrangements that cannot be changed easily; standardisation of accommodation and transport; limitation of contacts with the host-country; and almost complete insulation from another culture.

Many travellers prefer to make their own arrangements, often with the help of a travel agent, and to pay for these in advance. They prefer the freedom of being on their own, of making such contacts as they wish with the people of the host-country, or experiencing another culture. They enjoy the security of knowing that they have already paid for their basic necessities. Generally, this travel-style is best suited to those who have special interests, who think of travel as discovery as well as sight-seeing, and who seek not only relaxation but also the stimulus of a new experience, new food-tastes, rhythms, smells, sights, art-forms, and excursions away from the beaten track.

Yet other travellers prefer a minimum of pre-arranged features. They enjoy greater flexibility and freedom of choice but with a dash of uncertainty, the Worcester sauce that adds zest to travel.

Resorts – many options

Being several islands in one, Jamaica offers an opportunity to have several holidays in one. The options are many: combining sea-coast and mountain resort; a 'natural' south coast holiday with the comfort and sophistication of Montego Bay; renewing oneself with the healing waters of spas such as the Milk River Spa and the mineral springs at Bath and Sans Souci, or with the healing natural beauty of Ocho Rios and Port Antonio;

The beach at Jamaica Inn, Ocho Rios

stepping back into the past of buccaneers in Port Royal, and of coffee planters in the Blue Mountains; getting an insight into the industrial forces that have changed Jamaica's economy by visiting the new bauxite shipping ports and modern sugar factories; tracking down exotic trees and shrubs in historic botanical gardens and in the collections of the Institute of Jamaica. The combinations are many and each adds to the flavour of the other.

Whatever the variations, certain features remain constant: a good climate; friendly people; quick contact with an office of the Jamaica Tourist Board; a reliable island-wide communication system; health services of international quality; personal security.

Hotels, guest houses, villas, apartments

There are no huge impersonal hotels. Jamaica's largest hotels have between two hundred and five hundred rooms; the medium-size hotels have from fifty to two hundred rooms; the small hotels have ten to fifty rooms. Size is not an index to quality. In general, all hotel rooms are well-furnished, air-conditioned, and have private baths. Sanitation is good. The water is safe to drink. The kitchens are clean and well-run.

'Larger hotels' offer one or more bars, a restaurant and coffee-shop, patio, large swimming pool, ample lounge accommodation; easy access to swimming, water sports and tennis: easy access to a golf-course; nightly entertainment and dancing; and special activities such as barbecues and beach parties. Most of them are situated on the beach. The smaller hotels and guest houses have more limited lounge accommodation and fewer activities. Most have easy access to a beach, to tennis and golf; most of them provide meals but with a more limited menu. Their rates are lower, their rooms comfortable and well-furnished, usually with private bath; service is good, with the personal attention that family-run small hotels offer. The difference between the two classes is one of scale rather than of quality.

Increasingly the trend is toward furnished apartments in apartment hotels or in condominiums. An increasingly large number of visitors prefer to rent efficiency apartments or small apartments that can accommodate a family. A combination of villa or apartment and a rented car gives maximum flexibility at the lowest cost.

It is an added attraction that maid services are often available.

There being such a wide range of choice, visitors should get as much information as possible about the hotel or apartment, its location, whether it is on or near the beach; how far it is from a shopping centre; the availability and cost of fresh vegetables; how far it is from the airport; whether there are arrangements with other hotels for dining or interchange of meals; how near it is to a bank or to medical facilities; and what credit cards are accepted. It is a serious offence under Jamaican law to make any purchases except in Jamaican dollars (J$); this includes taxi fares, tips, car rental charges.

Whatever the option chosen, or the type of accommodation requested, the questions about cost should all be cleared up. Few things exasperate a visitor more than having to meet unexpected charges. For example, many countries charge a tax on hotel rooms. In Jamaica, check on the tax for the room. Does the rate quoted to you, the visitor, include this charge or not? There is also a departure tax of J$20 when you are leaving the country. Does the money paid for travel include this? Find out from the taxi driver what he is going to charge before getting into the cab.

JAVA, the Hotel Association, the local office of the Tourist Board and the staff of the hotel or guest house can assist with answers to these questions.

Clothing

Jamaica has a Mediterranean-type climate, so one dresses for coolness rather than for warmth. On the north coast the temperatures run from 80–88°F for most of the year. It is cooler in the winter season, October to March, when the temperature is in the late 70's. It can, however, be cold in the mountains, even in the summer, with temperatures that get down to the 40's. May and June, October and November are the wettest months.

Women favour cotton prints and fabrics that include some cotton, for coolness and comfort. A light raincoat and summer-weight pullovers and sweaters are always useful; also a light-weight folding umbrella; as many pieces of swim-wear as desired; casuals, shorts, slacks. Dark glasses are essential. Straw hats are best bought locally; they are well-made, have suitably wide brims and cost little.

Health and medication

Jamaica is a healthy country, with an excellent public health service. It is free from many of the diseases that afflict tropical countries. In the 1920's and 1930's the Government, with the help of the Rockefeller Foundation, wiped out hookworm by means of an intensive eradication programme. In the 1930's and 1940's tuberculosis was eradicated. An island-wide system of water purification, including filtering, chlorination and the provision of piped water, has eliminated typhoid. It is safe to drink the water from the tap. Malaria is controlled by a spraying programme.

The drive now is to improve the health care for pregnant and lactating women and malnourished children. There is a programme for children under two, involving immunisation against tuberculosis, diphtheria, poliomyelitis, tetanus and measles. International organisations and the development agencies of a number of countries have been supplementing the efforts of the Government and the Jamaican community to keep public health at its present high level. Involved in this effort is the University of the West Indies, whose medical school has an excellent international reputation. It trains doctors, carries out research and works closely with the island medical service. There are twenty-six public hospitals and in every major centre there are a number of well-qualified doctors.

Visitors on medication, and those who need to have prescribed medicines at hand should obtain from their doctors a letter of reference for the use of any local physician whom they might wish to consult. Pharmacists dispense drugs only on the prescription of a local doctor. Hotels usually have one or more doctors on call.

Hard drugs and marijuana (ganga) are illegal. Penalties for breaking the law are severe. This applies to the use of drugs and to having drugs in one's possession.

Investment and business contacts

The Government aims at attracting investors, and maintains offices of the Jamaica National Investment Promotion Ltd. in the United States, Canada and Western Europe so that would-be investors might have up-to-date information about business opportunities in Jamaica, government incentive legislation, and about the existing infra-structure of financial and professional institutions.

Jamaica National Investment Promotion Ltd. has offices at

New York	866 Second Avenue, 6th Floor, N.Y. 10017
Miami	25 S.E. 2nd Avenue, Suite 810, Miami, Florida 33131
Toronto	214 King Street West, Suite 216, Toronto, Ontario M5H 1K4
London	Trade Commissioner, 50 St James Street, London S.W. 1.

Airlines

Among the airlines serving Jamaica are Air Jamaica, Air Canada, British Airways, British West Indian Airways (BWIA), Eastern, Air Florida, American, Cubana, Viasa.

Air Jamaica, the national airline, serves New York, Toronto, Chicago, Philadelphia, Miami, San Juan, Port Au Prince and George Town (the capital of the Cayman Islands). Its 'Love Bird' service is popular with travellers, and it has established a remarkable safety record.

Travel documents

Vaccination certificates are required only from those coming from the Indian sub-continent, Central African countries and French territories of the Afars. They are not required for re-entry from Jamaica into the United States, Canada, the United Kingdom or Western Europe.

Passports are not required from citizens of the United States or Canada for visits of under six months, but they must have **proof of citizenship** or of **residence**, such as a passport, birth certificate, voter's registration card or naturalisation papers. Citizens of the United States and Canada do not require visas. Visas are not required by citizens of Commonwealth countries for visits of under six months, nor by citizens of West Germany, Austria, Switzerland, Sweden, Norway, Denmark, Italy, France or Holland for visits of under three months. In all cases, visitors must have with them the documentation required for entry into the country to which they are going after leaving Jamaica. These regulations apply to children as well as to adults.

Immigration and Customs

Forms and procedures are kept to the minimum. Visitors are required to fill in a form for entry into Jamaica. This has a carbon duplicate attached. The immigration office will hand back the duplicate, which should be kept safely with other travel documents since it will be required on departure.

The Customs declaration form is similar to that used in the United States.

The following items are allowed in duty free:

Personal belongings, 25 cigars, 200 cigarettes, 1 pint of liquor (no rum is allowed), ½ lb of tobacco and 1 quart of wine.

All goods other than these are dutiable.

The Government of Jamaica has placed a ban on the following:

Guns, hard drugs and marijuana, the importation or export of Jamaican currency, and on flowers, fruits and meat (unless canned).

This ban is necessary in order to keep the island free of foot and mouth disease. The island is also free of rabies, so there are restrictions on the importation of dogs and cats. These may be imported from the United Kingdom, Eire and North Ireland, but only with the necessary health certificates and with a permit from the Jamaica Ministry of Agriculture. This permit must be obtained in advance.

Currency regulations

The immigration card asks visitors and returning residents to state the amount of foreign and Jamaican currency they have with them. Any amount of foreign currency may be brought in but it is against Jamaican law to import or take out Jamaican currency.

Jamaican law requires that in Jamaica you use Jamaican currency. On arrival, convert some of your cash or travellers checks into Jamaican dollars at the airport terminal or at recognised Exchange Bureaux or at a bank. All charges must be paid for in Jamaican currency.

Credit cards may be used wherever they are honoured.

Charges will be made in J$ and the credit card company will make the conversion on payment.

The official rate of exchange varies from week to week as it does throughout the world. The official rates of exchange for major currencies is posted at Exchange Bureaux and Banks.

The bank or Exchange Bureau that changes the money will give a receipt for it. This should be kept safely since it enables a visitor to reconvert surplus Jamaican currency when leaving the island.

Jamaica Tourist Board Offices

Headquarters: New Kingston Hotel, Knutsford Blvd, Kingston 5.

Other offices

Chicago, Illinois	Suite 1210, 36 South Wabash Ave, Chicago, Illinois 60603
London, England	Jamaica House, 50 St James Street,
Mexico City, Mexico	c/o Mexicana Airlines, 36 Balderas, Mexico City, Mexico
Miami, Florida	320 South Dixie Highway, Coral Gables, Florida 33146
New York, N.Y.	866 Second Avenue, 10th Floor, New York, N.Y. 10017
Toronto, Canada	Suite 507, 221 Yonge Street, Toronto, Ontario, Canada M4S 2B4

Montego Bay	Cornwall Beach	tel: 952-4425
	Gloucester Avenue	952-4426
	Airport	952-3009
		or 952-2462
	Special Projects Dept.	
	Gloucester Avenue	
	Visitor's Service Bureau	
	General Manager, Cornwall Beach	952-2091
	Resident Manager,	
	Cornwall Beach	952-3734

Negril	Visitor's Service Bureau	957-4243
Ocho Rios	Pineapple Place	974-2570
	Special Projects	974-2684
Port Antonio	Rafters Rest	993-2778
	Dolphin Bay	993-2664

In bond or free port shopping

The important thing to remember is that in Jamaica only Jamaican currency is legal tender. This means that all 'in bond' or 'duty free' purchases must be paid for in Jamaican currency. Bear in mind that any liquor or tobacco purchased must be sent by the seller to the delivery counter at the international airport from which you are leaving. Often, in other cases, you may take delivery of other 'in bond' or 'duty free' purchases or you may direct that these also be sent to the delivery counter at the airport.

If you are **a United States citizen** you can take US $300 worth of goods (based on fair retail value) after staying for 48 hours outside the United States. Members of family, including infants, may combine exemptions. Declarations may be made by one member. Above this amount duty may be charged.

If you are over 21 years of age, you may take with you one quart (32 oz.) of alcoholic beverage. Above this quantity, duty will be charged.

You are allowed to mail to the United States **gifts** valued up to US $10 (fair retail value) free of US duty, but these gifts **must not** include liquor, perfume, cigars and cigarettes. The gifts will not affect the US $300 exemption.

Free port stores will attend to the mailing. You are allowed to mail an unlimited number of such duty free gifts, provided that the addressee does not receive more than US $10 worth in one day.

If you are a **Canadian citizen**, you are allowed to take to Canada US $10 worth of goods after you have stayed 48 hours outside Canada, free of Canadian duty. The accumulated value of such goods cannot exceed US $50 per calendar quarter. Excess (but only up to US $150) is subject to 25 per cent duty. After 7 days' absence, goods valued at US $150 can be brought in duty free once each calendar year.

9) Montego Bay and its surroundings

General information

The city of Montego Bay stands on a bay with the same name on the north-west coast of Jamaica, 18.28° latitude, 77.57° longitude. By air it is twenty minutes from Kingston, by rail 113 miles and by the A1 north coast road 120 miles. There is little elbow-room for the city between the sea and a huddle of high hills behind.

With a population of 30 000, Montego Bay is second to Kingston in size (but, claim Montegonians, second in nothing else). It is the capital of the parish of St James (240 square miles) as well as the commercial and administrative capital of the county of Cornwall, which includes the parishes of Hanover (177 square miles) and Westmoreland (240 square miles). It has a deep water pier with berthing for four vessels, a free port area and the facilities of a modern city.

The Bay of Good Weather – Golfo de buen Tiempo – was the name Columbus gave to the bay when he discovered it on 9 May, 1494. Spanish settlers moved to the island in small numbers after 1510, settling first on the north coast around Seville, near St Ann's Bay. They brought with them cattle, horses and pigs, which were left to roam wild on the savannahs and multiplied prodigiously. In time sloops and schooners began to call at Montego Bay for supplies of lard and hides; goods much in demand in a Europe that depended on candles for its lighting and on leather jerkins and boots for its armies. The Spanish for 'lard' being 'manteca', the bay was called Manteca Bahia; less romantic, but easier to say, than the name

105

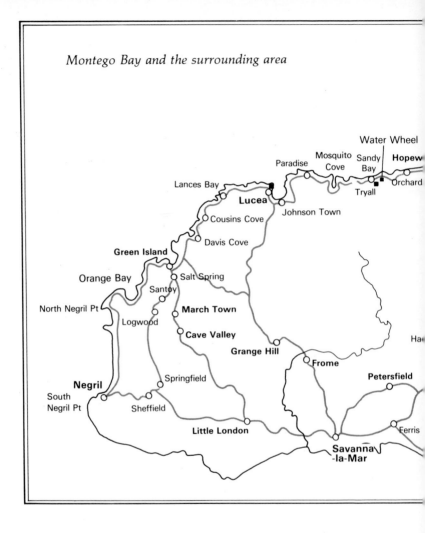

Montego Bay and the surrounding area

Water Wheel

Mosquito Cove Sandy Bay **Hopew**

Paradise

Lucea

Lances Bay

Orchard

Tryall

Johnson Town

Cousins Cove

Davis Cove

Green Island

Orange Bay

Salt Spring

Santoy

North Negril Pt

March Town

Logwood

Cave Valley

Grange Hill

Ha

Frome

Negril

Springfield

Petersfield

South Negril Pt

Sheffield

Little London

Ferris

Savanna-la-Mar

Columbus gave it. Some of the English, who took the island from Spain in 1655, settled around Manteca Bahia and, in the prosaic mood of those who named Rum Cay and Magotty, they called it Lard Bay. By good fortune the Spanish form prevailed and it became Montego Bay.

Allowing for growth and for the changes wrought by modern technology, the general impression of the city and its setting is much the same today as it was in 1802 when Maria Nugent, wife of the Governor of Jamaica, visited it.

106

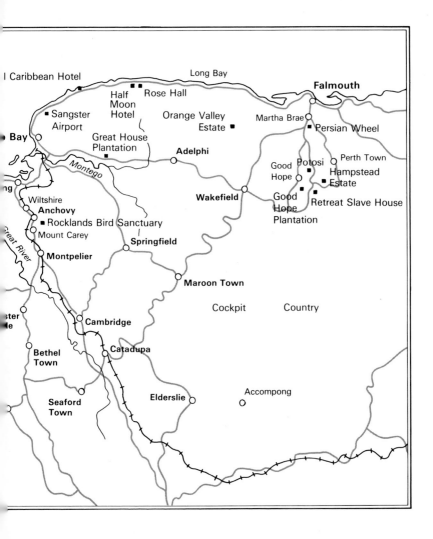

The town of Montego Bay is situated in an amphitheatre of
very high hills. In front a most beautiful bay, full of vessels
and open to the sea. On the hills are all the gentlemen's
houses, or those not immediately shopkeepers. These are
interspersed with gardens, palms, etc of all sorts. So that
from the town, quite up to the tops of the hills, you see
nothing but villas peeping out from among the foliage. . . .

Reading the landscape, we find sugar-cane on the flat land to
the east, in the direction of Falmouth and also to the immediate

west of the city. To the west also, in the direction of Lucea, are bananas and coconuts. Behind, on the terraces and in the valleys of the escarpment, are bananas and citrus.

Buses and trucks hurtle along the coastal highways and the roads that lead down the escarpment, to unload passengers and produce at the city market and city centre. Visitors from cruise ships and hotels mingle with city dwellers on the streets, or loiter at wayside stalls. Montego Bay is market town, commercial centre and tourist resort and its colourful, agitated life signifies a natural blending of country and city, foreign and indigenous.

To this movement in space let us add another dimension, that of time. This dynamic intermingling grew out of relationships between North America and the island that began when both were young.

Some of the ships that Maria Nugent saw in Montego Bay Harbour were from the eastern ports of the United States: Wilmington, Savannah, Charleston, Boston, and probably also from Halifax in Canada. The island had molasses and rum, which the North American colonies needed, and which they used in part for their fur trade with the Indians. In exchange, the northern colonies provided the islands with flour, salted meat and cod, staves for puncheons, nails, candles, horses and other plantation supplies.

The North American trade routes to the Caribbean were vital arteries. When they were cut, people in the islands died. Between 1773 and 1783 the slave population of Barbados fell from 68 000 to 57 400 largely as a result of famine caused by the interruption of the trade. Jamaica also suffered great distress during the same period.

People and ideas moved, as well as goods. George Washington's brother spent a year in Barbados trying to regain his health. When Benjamin Franklin was establishing the Academy in Philadelphia he sent Dr Howell to the sugar islands to collect money. Alexander Hamilton, who knew a good thing when he saw it, was taken at an early age from Nevis to the United States. Between 1650 and 1790 there were at least eighteen West Indian and Bermudan students at such colleges as Harvard, William and Mary and King's College in New York. In 1720 a Jamaica-born Jew was lecturer in Hebrew at Harvard. In addition there were close family ties between scores of families in the United States and the West Indies.

It is worth looking more closely at one example of the many far-reaching results of this Caribbean-North American relationship, one that involved Montego Bay and profoundly affected Jamaica.

At the outbreak of the American War of Independence a number of loyalist families moved to Jamaica. Some were slave-owners. One was the master of George Lisle, who was permitted to preach, and who converted Moses Baker, the slave of another loyalist immigrant. Lisle set up a chapel in Kingston, and Baker and himself soon had more church members than they could serve. In search of help, they appealed to the Baptist Missionary Society in London and in response the Society sent out its first missionaries to Jamaica in 1814. Methodist missionaries soon followed.

In Montego Bay, at the corner of Market Street and King Street, is the Burchell Memorial Baptist Church, named after Thomas Burchell (1799–1846), one of these pioneer missionaries. Another pioneer missionary was William Knibb, whose name lives in the William Knibb Memorial Church in Falmouth, at the corner of George Street and King Street.

The preaching of the native Baptists, Lisle and Baker, and of the missionaries, was dynamite. They were bitterly opposed by the planters, who understood very well that to preach that all men are the sons of God was to set in motion dangerous ideas about freedom and equality.

The message lodged in the heart of a domestic slave, Samuel Sharp, who lived in Montego Bay and was one of the members of Thomas Burchell's church. Literate, intelligent and a powerful orator, he found an outlet for his gifts in a mission church and built up an independent connection with the native Baptists who looked on him as their ruler or 'Daddy'. His reading of the Bible, the news of the emancipation movement in England and the American declaration that men are created free and equal convinced him that the slaves should make a bid for freedom. He called for a non-violent bid in which lives would not be taken.

On Tuesday, 27 December, 1831, a fire on Kensington Estate in St James marked the beginning of a slave rebellion which swept the western parishes and which is called, in Jamaica, the Baptist War.

The slaves indulged in widespread destruction of property but there is no hint of a crusade against the whites. There were only two crimes of violence against white people throughout the rising. A Presbyterian parson testified 'Had masters, when they got the better hand, been as forbearing, as tender of their slaves' lives as their slaves had been of theirs, it would have been to their lasting honour ...' They were not. They shot or killed two hundred and seven slaves and executed another three hundred and seventeen.

Daddy Sharp showed his genius by fastening on the one easily understood method: let every slave peacefully withdraw his labour. Gandhi and Martin Luther King were to employ this method of non-violence more than a century later. It is a measure of Sam Sharp's greatness that he fashioned this instrument against oppression. Sam Sharp was hanged. He told his friend, the Methodist missionary Bleby, 'I rather die than be a slave.' He is one of the national heroes of independent Jamaica, and belongs to that great company of men and women of all nations and tongues who made freedom a part of our heritage.

The Cage that stands at the north-west corner of Charles Square, the old Courthouse on its west side, and the Brandon Hill Cave are reminders of the past and of Sam Sharp's affirmation of freedom. The Samuel Sharp Training College is his memorial. For Jamaicans, Montego Bay is more than a resort or commercial centre. It is one of the national shrines of Jamaica.

Now for the city

West Indian cities have had more than their share of fires and hurricanes; after these have come a deluge of developers who tear down the past to build the latest concrete cliché. Even so, places still survive where we can touch the past.

Charles Square, or the Parade, was laid out in honour of the island's Governor, Admiral Charles Knowles. The place, like the heart of the city, is tight-squeezed; but there is a hint of graciousness.

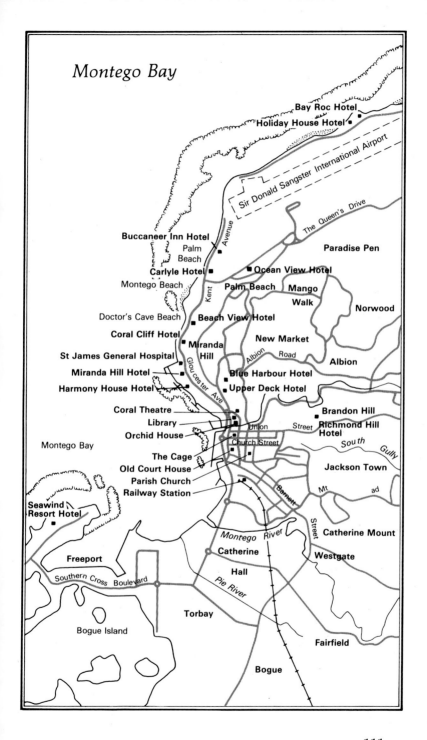

Montego Bay

Bay Roc Hotel
Holiday House Hotel
Sir Donald Sangster International Airport
The Queen's Drive
Buccaneer Inn Hotel
Palm Beach
Avenue
Paradise Pen
Carlyle Hotel
Ocean View Hotel
Montego Beach
Kent
Palm Beach
Mango Walk
Norwood
Doctor's Cave Beach
Beach View Hotel
Coral Cliff Hotel
Miranda Hill
New Market
St James General Hospital
Albion Road
Albion
Miranda Hill Hotel
Gloucester Ave
Blue Harbour Hotel
Harmony House Hotel
Upper Deck Hotel
Coral Theatre
Brandon Hill
Library
Union Street
Richmond Hill Hotel
Orchid House
South Gully
The Cage
Church Street
Old Court House
Jackson Town
Parish Church
Railway Station
Mt ad
Barnett
Seawind Resort Hotel
Catherine Mount
Street
Montego Bay
Montego River
Catherine
Westgate
Freeport
Hall
Southern Cross Boulevard
Pie River
Bogue Island
Torbay
Fairfield
Bogue

The Old Court House stood on the west side of the square. For Jamaicans it is a place of shadows and pain. Here brutal George Gordon, captain of the local militia, presided over a court martial after the 1832 slave rising and sentenced hundreds to beatings and hanging.

At the north-west corner of the square there is a small building, The Cage, with a cupola, dated 1806, which was once used as a lock-up for runaway slaves, disorderly seamen and vagrants. Sunday was market day for the plantation slaves, when they came into town to sell their produce. At two pm the constable rang a bell to warn the country slaves to leave the city. He rang the bell again at three pm as a last warning. After that any slave found on the streets was put in 'The Cage'.

The Dome has more pleasant and romantic associations. Legend tells how a Spanish girl and her little slave companion were playing near the Dome, by a stream that supplied the town with water. They were hunting crabs out of their holes. The Spanish girl moved a stone under which a crab had scuttled and heard the sound of bubbling water. So did the little slave. Frightened, they ran off to tell what they had heard. Half-believing, a few grown-ups went to the place, dug and found a spring. Delighted at finding this new source of fresh water, they freed the little slave and built the Dome to shelter the spring, which they called 'El Rio Camarones', Crab River. The present tower was built in 1837. The spring ceased being the town's source of water at the end of the last century.

Shopping is concentrated at the City Centre, where many of the in-bond shops are: Overton Plaza, the Holiday Village Shopping Centre where the Blue Mountains Gem Workshop invites visitors to see how the semi-precious stones are processed, and the Westgate Shopping Plaza. There are in-bond shops also at many hotels. Along Gloucester Avenue there are many booths with large assortments of Jamaican straw goods.

There are two places that should not be missed. One is the St James Parish Church, the city's great treasure. Cruciform, its foundations date back to 1778. In 1957 an earthquake destroyed the tower and so severely damaged the building that it had to be almost entirely rebuilt. This was done very skilfully, with very little change from the original. Pause for a minute or two to admire the limestone ashlar and the large round-headed windows that light up the interior so effectively, the mahogany fittings, the monuments which date back to the rich days of the plantocracy. The two most interesting are of Mrs Rosa Palmer, who should not be confused with the White Witch of Rose Hall, and Dr George McFarquhar. They are by John Bacon (1740–1799), the most celebrated English sculptor of his time, whose work also includes the Rodney monument in the square in Spanish Town.

The other is the market on Fustic Street. Europe touches Jamaica in the Parish Church, Africa in the market, with its 'enveloping sensory profusion and confusion'. Walking through these Jamaica markets, whether here or in Ocho Rios or Browns Town, it is possible to imagine oneself in the Yoruba and Ibo markets of Nigeria, which Wole Soyinka, Nigeria's great novelist, so vividly recreates; colourful markets, aroma-laden, markets such as one finds throughout West Africa, where sights and sounds blend together to form part of the country, the people, the past and the future, and to link together the three worlds that are for Africa one world, the ancestors, the unborn and the living. Here, instead of African fried bean cakes (akara) filled with green and red peppers and ground and chopped crayfish, there are fried fish, johnny cakes and bammies. The meats are different but the ritual is much the same, the reliving of a drama that was not cut short by a forcible transplanting from Africa to the Americas.

Excursions: Cornwall Beach

Cornwall Beach offers an underwater marine park; a long beach of white sand dotted with cabanas; water sports, scuba diving, snorkeling; a craft training centre where you can watch articles being made from straw and wood; a bar and cafeteria. On Friday evenings there is a beach party, which starts at seven pm with a barbecue, open bar, limbo, fire-eating, singing and dancing. On Saturday evenings there is a Jonkanoo Beach Party with performances by masked dancers, limbo dancers, calypsos, dancing, and with goat and donkey races. The entrance fee covers the cost of a buffet supper and drinks at an open bar.

A harbour cruise

The *Anne Bonney* offers an opportunity to see the city from the harbour at sunset, and to pick out some of the landmarks from the sea. The Freeport on the western side of the bay was made by reclaiming land and linking together a chain of mangrove-covered pancakes of land, known as the Bogue Islands.

The cruise takes two and a half hours. Call 952-9863 for information and reservations.

Evening on the Great River

This is fun, even though a mixture of natural charm and contrived amusement. The river setting is dramatic, for the trip is made at night in fishing boats manned by expert boat men, who take their passengers up a torch-lit river to an Arawak-style village. This has an open bar, dancing, floor show and features an 'old-time Jamaica country shop' that sells 'Jackass rope', which is cured leaf tobacco woven like a rope and sold by the inch or yard. It is pungent stuff. Other items for sale include cinnamon, spices and brown sugar.

Rocklands Bird Sanctuary near Anchovy

This excursion is recommended. The drive to Rocklands is an introduction to the natural beauty of rural Jamaica. The sanctuary is the life-work of a Jamaican, Lisa Salmon, internationally known as an ornithologist, who has created a sanctuary not only for birds but also for all people who find refreshment in nature, in birds, plants and gardens.

The sanctuary opens at half-past three in the afternoon. From then until dark is feeding time for the birds, and the porch of the house and the lawn are gay with the colour and movement of Jamaican humming birds, saffron finches, orange quits, the red-capped woodpecker and ground doves of soft slate gray. More than a hundred varieties of birds have been reported in the neighbourhood. Walks can be arranged for those who wish to explore further. Bird watchers or not, all visitors will find delight in the Forest Garden with its bird baths, ferns and shade plants of many kinds.

To get to Rocklands take the main road that leads from the city centre in the direction of Reading and Lucea.

At the junction to Reading, 4.8 miles west of Montego Bay,

Feeding a humming bird at the Rocklands Bird Sanctuary

leave the coast road, turn left up Long Hill, on the road leading to Anchovy, and continue for 2.2 miles up the escarpment.

At the top of the hill look for the signpost for Rocklands on the left. You will come to Rocklands Bird Feeding Station half a mile further on, on the right.

Returning by the same route, you will enjoy the view of Montego Bay as you descend Long Hill.

One-day tours

The **Governor's coach tour** to Appleton is made by rail. Details should be checked with the Jamaica Tourist Board.

The other tours described here lie in the same general direction, east of Montego Bay, and are reached by the north coast highway, A1. It is therefore possible to combine some of the tours, for example, the tour of the Great Houses, with Falmouth and Oyster Bay; or the Great Houses and the Martha Brae. Good Hope and the Windsor Cave will take a full day. Possible combinations and the length of time should be checked with a tour operator or the Jamaica Tourist Board.

Great House tour

This tour can be combined with a visit to Falmouth and Oyster Bay and with rafting on the Martha Brae. Take the north coast road (A1) and travel east to the **Rose Hall Great House**, passing Ironshore Estate and the Rose Hall Golf Course. It is nine miles from Montego Bay. The House was built between 1770 and 1780 by John Palmer, at the time Custos of St James, at a cost of £30 000. It consisted of a rectangular building three storeys high with two wings of one storey each that enclosed a courtyard at the back. The interior was beautifully panelled in mahogany, cedar and rosewood. The north coast was open to attack by privateers in war-time, and John Palmer protected his new home with a small battery of guns, wisely so, for in January 1780 he was able to scare off a Yankee privateer, the '*Tarter* of Boston, commanded by one Porter ... she mounts 18 6-pounders on one deck, six smaller on the quarter deck and carries 118 men ...'.

John Palmer lived beyond his means and had to mortgage Rose Hall a few years before his death. His grand-nephew John Rose Palmer inherited the property and lived there from 1820 to 1827, when he died.

The first mistress of the Great House was Rose Palmer who survived three husbands before marrying John Palmer. They lived happily together for twenty-three years. On her death John Palmer commissioned Bacon to carve her profile on the

Rose Hall Great House

monument in the St James Parish Church. This was the virtuous Mrs Palmer, whose manners were 'open, cheerful and agreeable', and who was 'warm in her attachment to her friends'.

In 1820 John Palmer's nephew, John Rose Palmer, brought his lovely young wife, Anne, to Rose Hall. Her beauty and wealth drew men to her, and her powers of witchcraft kept her terrified slaves submissive in spite of dreadful beatings and the agony of iron collars and spikes put on in her presence. After John's death in 1828 – who knows how? – she entrapped as lovers the book-keepers and overseers here and at Palmyra, and slaves as well, putting each to death when she tired of him. Whispers spread of bloodstains on the floor of an upstairs bedroom where a man died from a dagger wound and of an underground passage that led to the sea.

117

When mistress tire of the man she love
She make those two black slaves go throttle them
Den drag dem down dat passage to de sea
An' throw them to the sharks – dem tell no tales.

Her slaves hated her but dared not touch her because of her power as an obeah-woman. At last one of her lovers, finding he was falling out of favour, strangled her. None of her own slaves would bury the body. Planters brought their coachmen from near-by estates, buried her and marked the place with a square pile of masonry.

In the 1930's the celebrated medium Mrs Garrett visited Rose Hall. She became greatly disturbed at a spot in the courtyard which she identified as the resting place of Anne Palmer; and she reported that Mrs Palmer told her no one would ever find happiness at Rose Hall.

The story is told with embellishments by De Lisser in the *White Witch of Rose Hall*, and by Shore and Stewart in their book *In Old St James*. In recent years an historian, Geoffrey Yates, traced the second Mrs Palmer to a respected and peaceful death-bed and burial in the parish churchyard, but the Witch lives on in Jamaica's best-known horror story.

Cinnamon Hill Great House, a private property, abuts Rose Hall on the east. It belonged to the Barrett family, one of whose ancestors was a private in the English army which, under General Venables, took Jamaica from Spain in 1655. Elizabeth Barrett married the poet Robert Browning in 1846, against the wishes of her tyrannical father, Edward Moulton Barrett, who is portrayed in 'The Barretts of Wimpole Street'. Edward and Samuel had a sister, Sarah, the little girl in Lawrence's famous painting 'Pinkie'. She died at the age of twelve. The painting is now in the Huntington Library in San Marino, California.

The Great House has been modernised, but it retains its 'cut wind', designed to break the force of hurricane winds, and hollowed out inside to form a vaulted shelter.

Greenwood House, fourteen miles from Montego Bay, dates back to the early 1800's, though with later modifications. It contains authentic furnishings and a valuable collection of 18th century musical instruments. The house is privately owned but its owners have opened it to the public.

Falmouth and the Martha Brae

Falmouth was once a busy sugar port, frequented by ships from Europe and North America, which called for the molasses and rum produced by eighty or more sugar estates. Traces of its past elegance remain in its Georgian buildings, Parish Church and the Palladian Court House with a double staircase.

Fires and hurricanes ravaged Falmouth from time to time, and a period of neglect set in after the decline of the plantation trade. But the town is rich in history. The William Knibb Memorial Church at the corner of Church and King Streets is named after William Knibb (1803–1845), son of a tailor of Kettering in the English county of Northamptonshire who came to Jamaica in 1825 as a missionary. After moving to Falmouth he earned the hostility of the planters because of his 'subversive' preaching to the slaves. During the slave rising of 1831 Knibb and other missionaries were arrested and sent to Montego Bay. Knibb made his way to England, gave evidence against the system of slavery before Parliamentary Committees, campaigned passionately for emancipation, returned to Falmouth in 1834, supervised the building of the first Church (later destroyed by fire) and celebrated the granting of complete freedom with a midnight service at which the emblems of slavery, the chain, whip and iron collar, were buried. The scene is portrayed on a marble panel at the east end of the church, with Knibb's head at the base. It also has the profiles of the leaders of the English emancipation movement, Wilberforce, Sturge and Granville Sharp. In the churchyard are memorials celebrating the abolition of slavery.

Oyster Bay, 1½ miles east of Falmouth, gets its name from small oysters that cling to the roots of the mangrove trees. It has two inns, Fisherman's Inn and Glistening Water, which serve meals. The Bay is remarkable for its phospherence which can be observed at night.

Martha Brae and Witchcraft A few houses 1¼ miles east of Falmouth, at the junction of a road to Duanvale, mark the site of the first capital of Trelawny, before the river silted up and Falmouth became the port.

Legend says the name Martha Brae is that of an old Arawak witch who knew of a gold mine by the river. Some Spaniards

119

tried to find out the location from her. Martha Brae took them into a cavern full of human skeletons. Suddenly the river changed its course, poured through the cave, drowned the Spaniards and blocked the entrance for ever. Today the river is kinder to visitors, offering them off-the-beaten-track excursions. It also offers glimpses of the past through its Persian Wheel, which once lifted water from the river and poured it into a raised trough that supplied Falmouth.

The Martha Brae contains fish: mullet in the dam above the Persian Wheel, and tarpon and snook lower down, near the mouth of the river. The 'locals' can advise on the best times for trying one's luck.

More popular than fishing is rafting on the river. Excursions start at the Martha Brae rafting village, three miles inland, where there is a bar with restaurant. The cost of a rafting trip is US $25, but prices should be checked with the Tourist Board or with JADCO. Arrangements can be made through them.

Good Hope and Windsor Cave

There is something satisfying in a harmony of man's buildings with nature's work. Good Hope is an excellent example, and a visit is recommended.

Proceed from Martha Brae for 1.6 miles to a point where the road branches. Take the road to Good Hope, which is on the left-hand side. After one mile, at a junction, take the unpaved road. It leads through some of the old Trelawny sugar estates: Potosi with its derelict sugar works and Retreat Great House a mile further on, with a row of twenty-five low, one-roomed huts built of stone on the side of the hill. At a distance of 4¼ miles from Martha Brae you will come to Hampstead Estate; then drive through an avenue of bamboos beyond the entrance to Wales Estate, to arrive at last at Good Hope, 5½ miles from the starting point at Martha Brae.

John Tharp (1744–1804) bought the property – 3000 acres – in 1767. The owner of a Hanover estate, he married the co-heiress of Potosi. Together they bought up the neighbouring properties, to the point where it was said that Tharp could ride from the north to the south coast of Jamaica without leaving his own land. That was an exaggeration, but those who stay at Good Hope and ride along the bridle trails will find boundary stones bearing dates which bear witness to Tharp's expanding empire. It is said that he owned 10 000 acres of land and 3000 slaves.

After John Tharp died, Good Hope fell on hard times. Sugar prices were low. The owners lived in England. The property was broken up and sold. It passed through the hands of people who had little interest in it. Finally, in 1912, a wealthy American banker, J F Thompson, bought it. He appreciated its historic value and its potential. His son, combining good taste with business acumen, turned Good Hope into a hotel; its present owner continues the tradition of good taste, a sense of history and gracious hospitality.

Look, first, at the buildings that make up the complex: the Great House, built about 1755, with a central block with high ceilings, and with wings on the left and right set at right angles, and a portico; a small two-storey counting house that is a gem; an ice house with a tablet recording when the estate was settled; and below the Great House the estate buildings, including a slave hospital, later used as an Anglican church, an estate office and a small building with a Palladian front that may have been used as a store. Having looked at all these, stand back and absorb the whole, including the sugar works on the bank of the river and the lovely old stone bridge. Buildings and landscape are in perfect harmony.

Look then at the superb example of the architecture of nature. Continue along the road to Wakefield and Sherwood Content and when the road branches, take the one on the left that leads to Windsor – not the road on the right that leads to the 'house in a hollow', or, in Welsh, Pantrepant.

You are now at the edge of the Cockpit Country. Drive for two miles through a narrow corridor of limestone to Windsor, now owned by the Kaiser Bauxite Company. After passing some Company houses you will come to a pleasant meadow ringed with vine-covered limestone cliffs. Old Windsor Great House stands in the centre. The path to Windsor Cave is about half a mile from the Great House to the right. Take the path that forks right, cross to the entrance of the cave by a wooden gangway, pass through the narrow entrance and enter a large gallery with stalactite formations and substantial traces of bat manure. The gallery leads on for two or three hundred yards to a large chamber with a vaulted ceiling. Only experienced cave-explorers and speleologists should go beyond this point. Beyond are side-passages, and a narrow main passage with a mud floor. This suddenly drops thirty feet down a cliff to the channel of a little stream. This is the source of the Martha Brae. Retrace your steps and take away with you the memory of a richly sculptured Jamaica of measureless caverns and sunless streams.

Western Jamaica: Montego Bay – Negril

A splendid round tour can be done in a day, from Montego Bay via Negril, Savanna-la-Mar and Montpelier, but it is most enjoyable when time permits a stop-over in Negril. By arranging for this, you can escape from clock-watching and find relaxation in nature-watching, calling in at Tryall, stopping to see the old fort that commands Lucea harbour, adjusting to the leisurely pace of Negril, enjoying a picnic lunch on the beach at Bluefields, and returning to Montego Bay or going on to Mandeville and Kingston.

If it is at all possible, get hold of a copy of *Exploring Jamaica* by Philip Wright and Paul White, published by Deutsch, London. It is comprehensive, well-researched, accurate and contains a store of information not easily available elsewhere.

Leave Montego Bay by the A1 highway which runs west through Reading, (4.8 miles). At Reading a main road leading inland to Montpelier and Anchovy branches off to the left. It is best to return by this road. Continue on the Lucea road (A1) past some attractive houses by the sea, the most interesting being Wharf House, once the warehouse for the Montpelier estate when it produced sugar. At the Great River (7.4 miles) you cross from the parish of St James into mountainous Hanover and come to **Round Hill Estate**, and one of Jamaica's great hotels, which takes its name from the estate. The Round Hill Hotel stands on a circular knob of land overlooking the sea, a landmark easily identified by those arriving by plane. The hotel opens only for the winter season.

Doctor's Cave Beach, Montego Bay

Tryall, (12.5 miles), has a hotel, an excellent golf course, and a number of private residences. The estate once produced sugar, and the old mill wheel of the sugar works has been restored. Some of the estate buildings were destroyed by the slaves during the Baptist War of 1832. The water wheel is turned by water brought by aqueducts and stone gutters. Here, and occasionally along the road, there are reminders of the days when energy was provided by water and wind, by aqueducts, water wheels and windmills.

Mosquito Cove (17.5 miles,) is occasionally used by visiting yachts. It penetrates almost a mile inland.

Lucea (25.6 miles) is the capital of Hanover. It was once a busy sugar-port, of sufficient importance to be protected by a fort; this was erected on a promontory commanding the entrance to the harbour. It was named Fort Charlotte, and is one of the best preserved of the north coast forts. The old barracks form part of Ruseau School, which provides education at secondary school level for children in the eleven to seventeen age range. The school is named after its founder, a French refugee, Martin Ruseau, who was so grateful for the security and kindness he found in Hanover that he left his estate for founding a free school in the parish. Hanover cherishes the memory of another name, Alexander Bustamante, its most distinguished son. Sir Alexander's name was originally Clarke, and his father, Robert Clarke was an overseer on **Blenheim Estate,** which is reached by a side road from **Davis Cove** (34.1 miles). Blenheim is now a land settlement. The overseers' house has been reconstructed and is now a national monument. Continue your journey by way of Green Island and Orange Bay to Negril.

Accommodation: hotels and guest houses

The Jamaica Tourist Board publishes annually a list of the hotels of Jamaica. These are listed alphabetically, by resort area. Each hotel is placed in one of three categories, A, B or C, according to the number of rooms and the range of amenities and services offered. Hotel rates are quoted. These are provided by the hotels for the winter season for each year in question.

Visitors are advised to verify the rates with the hotels under consideration. Where there is any discrepancy, the applicable rate will be that posted by the hotel in its rooms and reception areas. All the rates shown here are daily per person unless otherwise stated.

The categories, A, B and C, enable visitors to pick out luxury, expensive and medium range or budget hotels and guest houses. They do not indicate deficiencies in the standard of accommodation or in services provided.

In most cases capsule descriptions are provided for hotels and guest houses in resort areas. In the case of Kingston this is abbreviated, to indicate some amenities and the location.

It is advisable to check with restaurants whether reservations are required for dinner, and whether dress is casual or not. Generally the cuisine is international, with a selection of Jamaican specialities.

EP indicates no meals;

CP breakfast only;

MAP breakfast and dinner;

AP three meals.

For your convenience the rates quoted here are in US currency. They are subject to change. Check the current rate of exchange for the Jamaican dollar, since this is the currency in which the hotel bills must be paid. As things are, the current rates are much in favour of visitors from North America and Western Europe. Check also on the amount of the accommodation tax, which is according to the category of hotel, and be quite clear as to whether this is included in the rates quoted to you.

Where two persons occupy one room, occupancy will be treated as one for tax purposes. Bills and receipts issued by the hotel should show the amount charged for accommodation separately from any amount charged for any other item.

Hotels and guest houses: Montego Bay

Beach View   Box 86, Montego Bay: (809)-952-4420/2   (C)
53 rooms, 140 beds: single $35–$40; double $22.50–$30 EP; private bath/shower; air-conditioning; rooms almost opposite Doctor's Cave, and near Cornwall Beach; pool on roof; patio area; pleasant and informal.

Blue Harbour   Box 212, Montego Bay: (809)-952-5445   (C)
22 rooms, 58 beds: single $36 EP; $40 CP; $57 MAP; double $22–$26, $25–$27, $42–$46; private bath/shower: air-conditioning; swimming pool; 10% added for gratuities.

Buccaneer Inn   Box 469, Montego Bay: (809)-952-2694   (C)
48 rooms, 150 beds: single $57 EP; double $33.5 EP private bath/shower; air-conditioning; cottages; beach rights; 10% added for gratuities; hotel in town at 7 Kent Avenue; close to beach.

Carlyle Beach   Box 412, Montego Bay: (809)-952-4140   (B)
52 rooms, 104 beds: single $61–$68; double $34.50–$37 EP; private bath/shower; air-conditioning; swiming pool, with hotel buildings grouped around; across road from ocean; pub bar.

Casa Montego   Box 161, Montego Bay: (809)-952-2450/5   (C)
129 rooms, 230 beds: single $68–$80, double $37–$43 EP; private bath/shower; air-conditioning; pool; cottages; 10% added for gratuities; night club; resort shops; beauty parlour; tennis; tour desk.

Chalet Caribe   Box 140, Montego Bay: (809)-952-1356   (C)
30 rooms, 70 beds: single $30–$40, double $18.50–$25 EP; private bath/shower; air-conditioning; swimming pool; private beach; 10% added for gratuities; water sports.

Chatham Beach   Box 300, Montego Bay: (809)-952-4780-1   (C)
100 rooms, 200 beds: single $66–$86; double $36–$40 EP; private bath/shower; air-conditioning; pool; private beach; 10% added for gratuities; orchestra; resort shops; beauty parlour; tennis; water sports.

Columbus Beach Hotel   Box 546, Montego Bay: (809)-952-4415   (C)
16 rooms, 40 beds: single $30–$35; double $22.50–$27.50 EP/CP; private bath/shower; air-conditioning; swimming pool; 10% gratuities added; tour desk.

Coral Cliff   Box 253, Montego Bay: (809)-952-4130/1   (C)
32 rooms, 64 beds: single $39–$49, double $19.50–$24.50; private bath/shower; air-conditioning; pool; 10% added for gratuities; tennis; tour desk; on edge of cliff; by sea.

Doctor's Cave Beach   Box 94, Montego Bay: (809)-952-4355   (C)
79 rooms, 150 beds: single $65–$70; double $47.50–$57.50 EP; private bath/shower; air-conditioning; pool; fishing; golf; private beach; 10% added for gratuities; night club; resort shops; beauty parlour; tennis; horseback riding; water sports; rooms on opposite side of road from Doctor's Cave beach, to which it has its own entrance.

Half Moon Club   Box 80, Montego Bay: (809)-953-2211   (A)
191 rooms, 400 beds: single $109–$239; EP, $189–$399 MAP; double $74.50–$139.50 EP, $114.50–$189.50 MAP: private bath/shower; air-conditioning; pool; cottages; fishing; golf; private beach; 10% added for gratuities; night club; orchestra; resort shops; beauty parlour; tennis; horseback riding; water sports; 1 mile east of Montego Bay on Ocho Rios road; Rose Hall Golf Club, 18 holes, across the road; spacious grounds; fronts on white sand beach.

Harmony House   Box 55, Montego Bay: (809)-952-5710   **(C)**
21 rooms, 42 beds: single $25–$29, double $19–$21 CP; private bath/shower; air-conditioning; pool; tour desk.
Holiday Inn   Box 480, Montego Bay: (809)-953-2485   **(B)**
522 rooms, 1000 beds: single $61–$76, double $33–$40.50 EP; private bath/shower; air-conditioning; pool; golf; private beach; 10% added for gratuities; night club; orchestra; beauty parlour; tennis; horseback riding; water sports.
Holiday House   Box 258, Montego Bay: (809)-952-2328   **(C)**
14 rooms, 32 beds: single $65, double $35 EP; private bath/shower; partial air-conditioning; pool; fishing; private beach; 10% added for gratuities; tennis.
Hotel Montego   Box 74, Montego Bay: (809)-952-3286/7   **(C)**
35 rooms, 88 beds: single $39–$55, double $22.50–$32.50 EP; private bath/shower; air-conditioning; pool; 10% added for gratuities.
Jack Tar, Montego Bay   Box 144, Montego Bay: (809)-952-4340   **(B)**
127 rooms, 254 beds: single $1048 weekly, double $799 weekly AP; private bath/shower; air-conditioning; pool; golf; private beach; resort shops; beauty parlour; tennis; water sports.
Kirlew Guest House   Box 182, Reading PO,
St James: (809)-952-1473   **(C)**
6 rooms, 10 beds: single $15, double $11 EP; private bath/shower; Reading is 3 miles west of Montego Bay.
Miranda Hill   Box 262, Montego Bay: (809)-952-3245/6   **(B)**
40 rooms, 80 beds: single $50, double $35 EP; private bath/shower; air-conditioning; pool; cottages; 10% added for gratuities; on hill overlooking bay.
Montego Bay Club Resort   Gloucester Avenue, White Sands PO,
Montego Bay: (809)-952-4310/5   **(B)**
90 rooms, 200 beds: single $65–$75, double $37–$43 EP; private bath/shower; air-conditioning; pool; beach rights; 10% added for gratuities; orchestra; beauty parlour; tennis; tour desk.
Montego Bay Racquet Club   Box 245, Montego Bay: (809)-952-1895
(telex 291915).   **(B)**
35 rooms, 60 beds: single $54–$60, double $30–$35 EP; private bath/shower; air-conditioning; pool; cottages; beach rights; 10% added for gratuities; tennis; tour desk; on hill overlooking bay; 7 hard tennis courts floodlit at night, tennis pro; free transportation to Doctor's Cave Beach.
Montego Gardens Apartments   Box 220, Montego Bay:
(809)-952-4838   **(C)**
24 rooms, 48 beds: single $42.50, double $21.25 EP; private bath/shower; partial air-conditioning; pool; 10% added for gratuities.
Mountainside Guest House   Box 1059, Montego Bay: (809)-952-4685
(telex 915 Mountainside)   **(C)**
5 rooms, 10 beds: single $17, double $12 EP; private bath/shower; partial air-conditioning; tour desk.

Ocean View　Box 210, Montego Bay: (809)-952-2662　　　　(C)
12 rooms, 25 beds: single $18, double $14–$15 EP; private bath/
shower; air-conditioning; 10% added for gratuities; tour desk.

The Palms　Rose Hall, PO Box 186, Montego Bay: (809)-953-2160 (A)
18 rooms, 54 beds: 2–6 persons, $105–280 EP; private bath/shower;
air-conditioning; pool; cottages; private beach; tour desk.

Richmond Hill Inn　Box 362, Montego Bay: (809)-952-3859
(telex MBJ 915)　　　　　　　　　　　　　　　　　　　　(B)
21 rooms, 31 beds: single $36 EP, double $23–$40 EP; private bath/
shower; air-conditioning; pool; fishing; 15% added for gratuities;
orchestra; beauty parlour; old plantation house overlooking bay.

Rosehall Beach and Country Club　Box 999, Montego Bay:
(809)-953-2650　　　　　　　　　　　　　　　　　　　　(A)
500 rooms, 960 beds: single $100–$120, double $50–$60 EP; private
bath/shower; air-conditioning; pool; fishing; golf; private beach;
10% added for gratuities; night club; orchestra; resort shops; beauty
parlour; tennis; horseback riding; water sports.

Round Hill　Box 64, Montego Bay: (809)-952-5150/5　　　(A)
101 rooms, 219 beds: $190–$310 single, MAP, $205–$325 AP; double
$122.50–$185.50 MAP, $137–$197.50 AP; private bath; air-
conditioning; swimming pool; cottages; fishing; golf; private beach;
orchestra; resort shops; beauty parlour; tennis; horseback riding;
water sports; on a 98 acre peninsula; one of the finest luxury hotels in
the Caribbean; main buildings front beach; villas in spacious grounds;
small sandy bay with terrace for informal luncheons; dress for dinner.

Royal Carribbean　Box 167, Montego Bay: (809)-953-2231
(telex 915 MOBAY)　　　　　　　　　　　　　　　　　　(A)
165 rooms, 330 beds: single $102–$286, double $54.50–$154 EP;
private bath/shower; air-conditioning; pool; fishing; private beach;
orchestra; resort shops; beauty parlour; tennis; water sports, two-
storey building on beach, plantation style, on eastern limits of
Montego Bay; near airport.

Royal Court　Box 195, Montego Bay: (809)-952-4531　　　(C)
22 rooms, 50 beds: single $30–$40, double $20–$34 EP; private bath/
shower; air-conditioning; pool; 10% added for gratuities; night club.

Sandals　Box 100, Montego Bay: (809)-952-5510
(telex 5333 Sandals JA)　　　　　　　　　　　　　　　　(A)
173 rooms, 173 beds: double $775.00–$1000 weekly AP; private
bath/shower; air-conditioning; pool; cottages; night club; orchestra;
tennis; private beach; water sports; villas on beach; hotel rooms face
sea.

Seawind Beach Resort　Box 1168, Montego Bay
Freeport: (809)-952-4874/4070/2 (telex MO PORT 5329)　　(C)
430 rooms, 860 beds: single $48–$80, double $31.50–$45 EP; private
bath/shower; air-conditioning; pool; cottages; private beach; 10%
added for gratuities; night club; orchestra; resort shops; tennis; horseback riding; water sports.

Toby Inn Box 467, Montego Bay: (809)-952-4370/1   (C)
28 rooms, 52 beds: single $40–$45, double $22.50–$25 EP; private
bath/shower; air-conditioning; pool; cottages; 10% added for
gratuities; night club/discotheque; within short walk of Doctor's Cave
Beach.
Trelawny Beach Box 54, Falmouth: (809)-954-2450/2470   (A)
350 rooms, 700 beds: single $97 MAP/$106 AP; double $76 MAP, $85
AP; private bath/shower; air-conditioning; pool; cottages; private
beach; beach rights; 10% added for gratuities; night club/
discotheque; orchestra; resort shops; beauty parlour; tennis;
horseback riding; water sports.
Tryall Golf and Beach Club Sandy Bay PO, Hanover:
(809)-952-5110/3   (A)
44 rooms, 88 beds: single $180–$220 (Nov 1-April 15) double
$105–$125 MAP; private bath/shower; air-conditioning; pool;
cottages; private beach; 10% added for gratuities; resort shops;
tennis; horseback riding; water sports; estate Great House forms
nucleus of hotel buildings; 12.6 miles from Montego Bay.
Upper Deck Box 16, Montego Bay: (809)-952-5120/3   (C)
109 rooms, 226 beds: single $78–$98, double $44–$55 EP; private
bath/shower; air-conditioning; pool; beach rights; resort shops; tour
desk; on hill overlooking bay; set in terraced gardens; six compounds
of rooms named after British admirals; rooms with kitchen.
Verney House Box 18, Montego Bay: (809)-952-4845/2875   (C)
29 rooms, 65 beds: single $20–$22.50, double $11.25–$12.50 EP;
private bath/shower; partially air-conditioned; pool; beach rights;
10% added for gratuities; tour desk.
Wexford Court Box 239, Montego Bay: (809)-952-3679/2854   (C)
38 rooms, 76 beds, single $50–$65, double $30-$42.50 EP; private
bath/shower; air-conditioning; pool; tour desk; near Doctor's Cave
Beach.

Restaurants and cafes not listed above

The specialties listed were correct at the time of going to press but
may, of course, change.
Brigadoon Restaurant (tel: (809)-952-1753): in Queen's Drive; offers
free transportation from and to hotel; open 5:00 pm to 1:00 am;
dining on half-covered patio, also dining-room; specialties include
Brigadoon conchfish starter with rum-garlic sauce, smoked dolphin;
main meal includes soup, salad, rolls and butter, with lobster dishes
–$18–$35; butterfly shrimp deep-fried, sirloin steak, chicken
tandoori. Dress informal; dancing.
Diplomat (tel: (809)-952-3353): also in Queen's Drive; gracious
surroundings.

Blackbeard's Tavern, Au Refuge, Lobster World (tel: (809)-952-3840): near Doctor's Cave; three restaurants as one; specialties lobster cocktail, pumpkin soup, stuffed baked lobster, lobster bombe and steaks; at Blackbeard's full fondue dinner.

Ramparts Inn (tel: (809)-952-4830): Queen's Drive and Leader Avenue; French cuisine; specialties include pumpkin soup with fresh cream; langoustines Provençales with tabasco; flambéed steak au poivre; desserts include banana flambé $2.30 and Ramparts Lime pie. Reservations required.

Calabash Restaurant (tel: (809)-952-3891): Queen's Drive near the Diplomat: dining on Garden Terrace overlooking bay; lunch from 12:00 to 2:30 pm; dinner starts at 6:00 pm; curried goat with rice; pork chops; hot-pot of beef in red wine sauce; ackee and salt-fish.

Jerk Pork Bar: on Kent Avenue, in open; Jamaican delicacy, highly seasoned barbecued ribs grilled over charcoal fire; jerk chicken. Prices shown on blackboard in hut.

Pelican Grill Gloucester Avenue; coffee-shop style; air-conditioned; omelettes, hamburgers, ham or bacon and eggs, fresh fruit salad; also Jamaican dishes.

Town House (tel: (809)-952-2660): old brick house on Church Street; bar and restaurant in refurbished air-conditioned cellars, lit with old ship's lanterns; specialties include Surf and Kebabs, barbecued spare-ribs with Tennessee sauce, stuffed lobster, red snapper en papillotte.

Chinese Restaurant (tel: (809)-952-3254): on Strand Street; with take-out service; dishes include sweet-and-sour pork with pineapple; special chow choy, pork and stuffed shrimp; chow mein; chop suey; seafood dishes. Upstairs Mackenzie's drug store, simply furnished, clean, reasonable prices.

ALSO:

Kentucky Fried Chicken, on Orange Street, near City Centre; offers 15 pieces plus rolls as family bucket.

Chicken Joint on Union Street at Overton Shopping Plaza, take-out and delivery service.

Butter Flake Pastry Shop on Union Street, sells famous Jamaican specialty, piping hot highly-spiced patties; other pastry shops also in town.

10 Negril, Savanna-la-Mar and Montego Bay

General information

The most westerly part of Jamaica is South Negril Point. From there the land sweeps gently north, to form Long Bay, with a seven mile stretch of sandy beach. North of Long Bay is Negril Harbour, sometimes called Bloody Bay, smaller and more sheltered.

Negril and Negril Beach are not on Negril Harbour but at the southern end of Long Bay, near the mouth of the Negril River, and north of Negril Hill. The resort is easily reached from Montego Bay, 48½ miles to the east, by the A1 highway which, after leaving Montego Bay, passes through Hopewell, Tryall, Lucea and Green Island. From Kingston it is 150 miles by the A2 highway, passing through Spanish Town, Mandeville and Savanna la Mar.

Negril is in the parish of Hanover (177 square miles), of which Lucea is the capital. The chief occupations are raising cattle and growing coconuts, pimento, ginger and ground provisions, including the highly-prized Lucea yam. Sugar estates and large plantations have not dominated the parish, largely because the terrain is so mountainous. As a result there has never been a strong commercial centre, and trade gravitated to Montego Bay. The Montego Bay people speak of their parish as 'noble St James' and the Hanover people speak of 'neglected' or 'forgotten Hanover'. The increasing popularity of Negril has changed that.

The two most striking physical features of Negril are its glorious seven-mile beach of white sand, surely the finest and safest in the world, and the Great Morass, a two mile wide

131

swamp for long a barrier in the way of development. In the 1960's the barrier was breached by an extensive drainage system based on a canal at the foot of the hills which carried the run-off water to the sea, and by canals through the swamp.

There are three sheltered bays: Long Bay, Bloody Bay (possibly because whales were once slaughtered here) and Green Bay. Just off the northern end of Long Bay is a delightful little island, named Booby Cay, now frequented by nude bathers.

The beach at the Negril Beach Village Hotel

The bay had strategic value in sailing-ship days though the Great Morass blocked its development as a port. It was used at times as a gathering point for convoys bound for England; it was from this bay that a British expedition sailed to attack New Orleans in 1814. The best-remembered name from those times is that of the pirate Jack Rackham, nicknamed Calico Jack because of his fondness for calico underclothes. For two or three years he plagued Jamaica's north coast, until Captain Barnet, in command of an armed sloop, surprised him and his crew at a rum-punch party on Negril Beach. Calico Jack and his crew were tried in Spanish Town. At the trial, two of the toughest members of the crew were found to be women, for 'they pleaded their bellies, being great with child'. One was Anne Bonney, Jack's mistress. The other was Mary Read, who was brought up as a boy and served with Marlborough's army in Flanders. Both were condemned to death. Mary died in prison from fever. Anne escaped punishment. Jack was executed. His body was put in an iron gibbet and hung on a small sandy cay outside Kingston Harbour, now called Rackham's Cay.

Today, the barrier of the Great Morass having been breached, roads, an air-strip and the telephone link Negril with the rest of Jamaica and the world. Jamaica, however, is many islands in one, each having its own character, its own moods and rhythms, and so each of the six major tourist resort areas differs from the others. Negril, for example, has no city or town base. A visitor who sets out from the Montego Bay airport finds himself, ten minutes later, landing on an air-strip near a sprawling village half-hidden by trees and shrubs, without a high-rise building in sight. It is easy for the people living in the small village of Green Island to relate as neighbours to the Negril visitors. The themes are neighbourliness and 'Enjoy Today', but in a relaxed way, with a minimum of formality and of clothing. The hotels, guest houses and apartments repeat this message with an emphasis on personal service in a country-inn atmosphere.

Hotels and guest houses

Charela Inn   Box 33, Negril: (809)-957-4277   (A)
10 rooms, 17 beds: single $100 MAP; double $67.50–$75 MAP; private bath/shower; air-conditioning; private beach; 10% added for gratuities. Sea front inn, Spanish hacienda style; family owned and run; variety of water sports; tennis; golf; excursions possible.
Coconut Grove   Box 12, Negril: (809)-957-4216   (A)
32 rooms, 88 beds: single $140; double $97.50 MAP; private bath/shower; air-conditioning; pool; fishing; private beach; 10% added for gratuities; orchestra; resort shops; tennis; horseback riding; water sports. Apartment hotel, on Long Bay Beach; wide range of sports and activities.

134

Hedonism 11   Box 25, Negril: (809)-957-4200 (telex MBJ 915)   **(A)**
280 rooms, 560 beds: single $770–$860 weekly, AP; private bath/
shower; air-conditioning; pool; private beach; night club/dis-
cotheque; resort shops; tennis; horseback riding; water sports.
Negril Beach Club   Box 7, Negril: (809)-957-4245   **(B)**
97 rooms, 200 beds: single $55–$87 EP; $77–$109 MAP; double
$30–$49.50 EP; $52–$71.50 MAP; private bath/shower; air-
conditioning; pool; private beach; 10% added for gratuities; night
club/discotheque; resort shops; tennis; horseback riding; water
sports.
Sundowner   Box 5, Negril: (809)-957-4225   **(A)**
26 rooms, 52 beds: single $85–$90; double $60–$65 MAP; private
bath/shower; air-conditioning; private beach; 10% added for
gratuities; resort shops; beachside two-storey building; owner-
managed; relaxed family-feel atmosphere.
T-Water Beach Hotel   Box 11, Negril: (809)-957-4270/1   **(C)**
60 rooms, 114 beds: double $27.50–$45 EP; private bath/shower; air-
conditioning; private beach; beach rights; 10% added for gratuities.
Wilton House   Box 20, Bluefields, Westmoreland, (809)-955-2852 **(C)**
4 rooms, 8 beds: single $45; double $40 MAP; private bath/shower;
fishing; private beach; beach rights; horseback riding; water sports.
Bluefields is 39 miles from Negril, on the south-west coast, 12 miles
east of Savanna-la-Mar.

Restaurants and cafés not listed above

Mariner's Inn   Open air dining; local specialties include fresh lobster,
snapper, Jamaica style chicken.
Rick's Cafe   Near Rockhouse; popular meeting place for 'sun-
downers' and watching the sun go down; lobster, omelettes, eggs
Benedict, hamburgers.
Sundowner   (tel: (809)-957-4225): For West Indian buffet, Jamaican
specialties; dinner under thatched roof beside beach.
Negril Sands Club   Seafood buffet lunch.
Breadbasket   In the shopping centre; good pastry.

Negril to Savanna-la-Mar and Montego Bay

From Negril it is worth returning to Montego Bay and
completing the western circuit by taking the A1 through
Savanna-la-Mar and then, turning left at Ferris Cross, driving
through pleasant inland country to Reading and Montego Bay.

Leaving Negril, travel east by way of Sheffield and Little London to Savanna-la-Mar, eighteen miles from Negril and thirty-three miles from Montego Bay by the B8. Savanna-la-Mar, often called Sav-la-Mar for short, is the capital of the parish of Westmoreland most of which, in contrast to Hanover, lies on a fertile alluvial plain and has several cattle ranches. The Frome Sugar Factory is five miles north of Savanna-la-Mar on the B9. The town has an unhappy record of destruction by hurricane and tidal wave. In 1780, during a hurricane, 'the sea rose, a mighty wave swept up the beach for nearly a mile, and, as it retired, left two ships and a schooner stranded among the trees.'

A Jamaican cattle ranch

Savanna-la-Mar was the home of a Church of England priest, the Revd Henry Clarke, (1820–1907), who identified himself with the great mass of Jamaicans, to the displeasure of the planters and Anglican clergy. At the time of the Morant Bay rising he protested strongly to the Anti-Slavery Society in England about the illegal execution of William George Gordon, and prophesied that Gordon would one day be honoured with a national monument. Henry Clarke took the lead in founding the Westmoreland Building Society, now the National Building Society, one of the strongest in the island. His family continued the tradition of public service through the late Edith Clarke, author and social worker, and Eric Clarke, formerly a Custos of the parish.

Manning's School, on the main road west of the Building Society's office on the corner of Beckford and Barracks Street, owes its beginnings to a Westmoreland planter, Thomas Manning, who left thirteen slaves, land and the produce of a pen and cattle to endow a free school. The school was founded in 1738, twenty-eight years after Manning's death. It has been greatly enlarged and now, like Ruseau's, holds an honoured place in the history of Jamaican education.

From Savanna-la-Mar drive east along the A2 to Ferris Cross (5 miles) and turn left through Whithorn (4 miles) to Haddo, home of Charles Stewart, one of Jamaica's many prophets, who was known as 'the prophet of Haddo'. He attracted a large following by his predictions. He built a shrine in the hills and a balm yard. The building is easily recognised by a white flag on a pole, often with a display of other flags also, where a 'balm man' or 'balm woman' practises herb-healing, folk-medicine and either obeah or myal healing, this last being against the law. Bush teas and 'fever baths' made with collections of herbs or 'bush' are essential parts of the process.

Knockalva, three miles beyond Haddo, is an agricultural training centre for a hundred youths of fifteen to nineteen. **Montpelier,** twenty miles from Savanna-la-Mar and just over eleven from Montego Bay, is one of the largest cattle properties in Jamaica.

Montpelier, Haddo and Mount Carey are counterpoints in the history of Jamaica. They symbolise the imported and the indigenous, scientific technology and folk-beliefs. The three places point to different, even opposed forces, which shaped Jamaica's way of life; they also point to the future, to Jamaica's capability for drawing on external sources of technology and capital without weakening its sense of national identity.

For one hundred and sixty years, from 1752 to 1912, Montpelier belonged to the Ellis family. This Jamaica connection dated back to the period of Charles II of Britain, when John Ellis came to the island and patented Ellis Caymanas near Spanish Town. A descendant, Charles Rose Ellis (1771–1845), was an absentee proprietor who lived in England and was one of the leaders of the West Indian interests there. He was raised to the peerage as Lord Seaford. After sugar prices fell in the 1840's, Montpelier switched to cattle, and was one of the pioneers in importing Mysore and Zebu cattle from India. These were able to withstand drought and heat. Experimental breeding was continued throughout the years and became a feature of the Montpelier-Shettlewood estates.

By chance, the Ellis family also had a hand in importing guinea grass, which provided better feed for the cattle. The captain of a slave ship brought in for Chief Justice Ellis some rare African birds and a bag of the seed on which they fed. The birds died. The bag with the seed was shaken out and forgotten. Some time afterwards the cattle were seen to be gathering at a particular place and enjoying an unknown grass. The African seed, guinea grass, was remembered and the place was fenced in; the grass spread and Jamaica gained a grass that for a long period sustained its cattle industry.

From Montpelier a road leads to Cambridge and Seaford Town, twelve miles away. The village is named after Lord Seaford, who gave five hundred acres of partially cleared land for settling a number of Germans who were brought in after emancipation to settle as peasant farmers. About two hundred and fifty of them settled but they had a difficult time. Some died, others emigrated. Today Seaford Town is an inbred dying community of fair-skinned, blue-eyed peasant farmers of German origin.

Mount Carey Baptist Church, twenty-two miles from Savanna-la-Mar and just over nine from Montego Bay, speaks of the struggle for emancipation and the work of Thomas Burchell, whose name is recorded on an obelisk, and William

Knibb. After the abolition of slavery in 1834 Thomas Burchell made his home here. Like the Webb Memorial Church in Falmouth and the Burchell Memorial Baptist Church in Montego Bay, Mount Carey is a reminder of the struggle of the people and of the missionaries to achieve freedom. Bethel Town, five miles from Mount Carey, is one of the free villages which Burchell founded after emancipation.

The prophet of Haddo should not be dismissed as 'superstitious' or 'mad'. He is one of a large company of shepherds and shepherdesses, preachers and prophets, balm-yard men and balm-yard women who became aware of, and sought to minister to, deep spiritual needs in the society. They had a sense of mission. Some were Messianic leaders to whom the folk immediately responded. Mount Carey, on the other hand, symbolises a struggle for, and the achievement of, freedom in the way that Sam Sharp does. It symbolises also a blend of 'native Baptist' with Christian missionary teaching and guidance. Montpelier, on the other hand, points to the value of external influences and knowledge for improving agricultural technology and strengthening the island's economy.

11 Ocho Rios and its surroundings

General information

Ocho Rios is on the north coast of Jamaica, midway between Montego Bay in the west (67 miles) and Port Antonio in the east (67 miles). It is sixty miles from Kingston, which lies to the south-east. A small country town, with a population of seven thousand, it stands on a semi-circular bay which has a deep water pier with berthing for two ships. The Reynolds Jamaica Mines Company ships bauxite from Ocho Rios to the United States. Their installations for storage and shipping are toward the western part of the bay.

As the map shows, it is easy to reach Ocho Rios from almost any part of Jamaica. Trans-Jamaica, Wings Jamaica and Jamaica Air Taxi use the Boscobel Airport, which is twenty minutes from the centre of town. The highway from Kingston, the A1, goes by way of Spanish Town and the Bog Walk Gorge to Moneague, where there is a junction with the A3. The shorter and more scenic route is by the A3 from Moneague by way of the Fern Gully to Ocho Rios.

The route from Montego Bay is by the A1, through Discovery Bay and St Ann's Bay by the A3, which continues beyond Ocho Rios, Port Maria and Annotto Bay to Port Antonio.

A network of roads links Ocho Rios with the towns and villages of Central Jamaica. There will be a description of some of these in the section on tours and excursions.

Ocho Rios is a happy place, secure in itself. It is not burdened with being the capital of a parish, like St Ann's Bay, seven miles

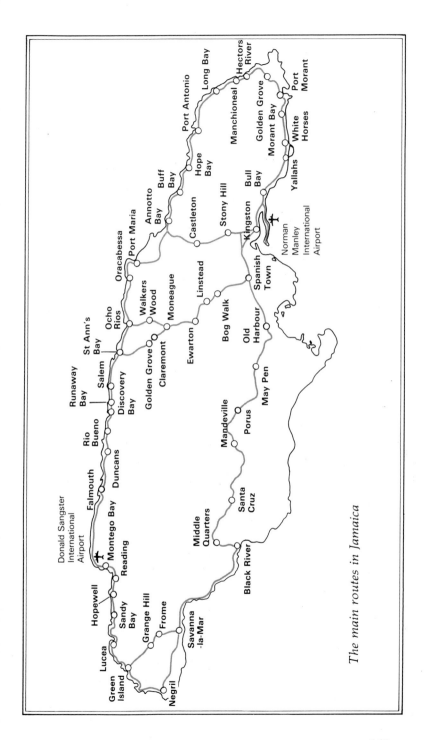

The main routes in Jamaica

to the west. It is neither a commercial nor an industrial centre, though Reynolds Jamaica Mines is only twelve miles away, at Lydford. It is a large resort but it is not dominated by hotels; they are strung out along forty miles of coast from the Jamaica Hilton in the west to Oracabessa, twenty-five miles to the east. The visual impact of a luxury development such as the Shaw Park Corniche, possibly the finest of its kind in Jamaica, or of the hotels and expensive villas that line the coast, is diminished by the fact that they all fit into a landscape of gardens; and these gardens 'belong'. They are not so manicured as to appear artificial. Jamaicans also belong here. They welcome visitors but they are the hosts.

The impact of Ocho Rios is immediate and affirmative without being assertive or aggressive. Pause at the wayside stalls that line the road from Pineapple Place to Jamaica Inn, or at the market in Ocho Rios, or at the little shops that sell Jamaica patties, curried goat, jerk pork, jerk chicken, sweet potato pone, and gizadas (which are flour shells filled with sweetened grated coconut). Home-made ginger beer performs the double function of calming the stomach and refreshing the body; at Christmas time, try the appetizer made from sorrel flavoured with ginger. Try roast corn on the cob and beef soup or goat-head soup. The indigenous is everywhere. It is not swept under the counter.

Give some time to the carvings especially. Most Jamaicans are descendants of African peoples, predominantly of the Akan-Ashanti people of Ghana and of the Ibo people of Nigeria. These, in common with so many other African peoples, have a long tradition of wood-carving. Haiti never forgot it. Jamaica did. A revival of spirit came with the national movement of the 1930's when Jamaica began to express itself in music, the dance, painting, carving and literature. There is an almost confusing profusion of work. The quality is uneven, but the discerning eye will find work of quality.

The unique 'feel' of Ocho Rios transmits itself not only through the people in the wayside markets and the country markets in Ocho Rios, Claremont, Browns Town and the rest, but also through attitudes. St Ann is known to all Jamaicans as the 'Garden Parish'. No other parish can make that claim. 'St Ann people' are proud of that.

The view over Ocho Rios from Shaw Park

One crystal morning I stood looking from a vantage point on the Chalky Hill road, tracing the contoured pattern from the fringe of offshore reef across the rim of plain to the upland terraces. The inevitable goat was there, tethered by the side of the road, for that is common property and why should the public grass not provide food for a private entrepreneur? It was so clear a morning that I almost persuaded myself the clouds on the distant horizon were the mountains of Oriente Province in Cuba.

Suddenly I became aware of someone approaching. It was an elderly woman, bony, as finely chiselled as an old pimento tree.

She spoke very quietly. 'Pretty, pretty for true, thank Massa God. I live here from when I was a little child and I never get tired of this. You know, I don't have no money, but this belong to me, to me and Massa God. Pretty for true.' She asked for nothing but the companionship of sharing this beauty.

This sense of identity, of belonging, has its roots also in ownership and in achievement. Bordering on the large properties, once wholly owned by whites, are the homes of middle-size farmers and smallholders whose three-tier cultivations have tall trees like breadfruit for food and shelter; coffee and citrus at a lower level; and ground provisions such as yams and sweet potatoes and the delicious small green cabbages that Jamaica grows so well. There are chickens, of course, and a pig, one or two goats and a cow that is tended by the family; as Jamaicans say, 'black man's cow knows hand, white man's cow knows rope'.

St Ann, like the other parishes, has its tradition of independence. Slavery was abolished in 1834, but a six-year system of forced labour, 'apprenticeship', was instituted. The resistance of the people brought it to an end in four years but the 'new frees' of St Ann rejected it from the start. Twenty-five years later, when three years of drought had burned the crops and low wages and unemployment had reduced the peasants to distress, one hundred and nine St Ann smallholders took the initiative and petitioned 'our most gracious Sovereign Queen Victoria rule over us, long may she live', telling of their condition. '... we are compelled to rent land from the large proprietors ... and the rent must be paid in advance.... We are far away from our Gracious Queen otherwise your humble servants would all speak to our Sovereign personally of our distress.' The petition was sent through Governor Eyre, who advised a reply so harsh that it helped to ignite the Morant Bay rising of 1865.

The feeling of achievement comes in part from knowing how well sons and daughters, cousins and nephews have done in the United States, Canada and England. In part, it also comes from the knowledge that a little boy, born near St Ann's Bay of a poor family, with only elementary school education, became the accepted leader of millions of black people in the United States and throughout the world. This was Marcus Garvey, 'Black Moses' as his biographer Cronin called him. They cherish, and identify with, Garvey's belief in the capacity of the black man to create and achieve on his own terms.

That belief was re-inforced by Bob Marley, St Ann's poor boy, whose reggae took the world by storm. Like Garvey, he was a world figure; and like Garvey, a St Ann boy who started with nothing more than his natural gifts.

The name Ocho Rios means 'Eight Rivers' but the name used even up to a century and a half ago was Las Chorrerras, the waterfalls, and this may have been corrupted to the present form. Either way, this part of the coast is blessed with streams and waterfalls, the best known being Dunns River Falls.

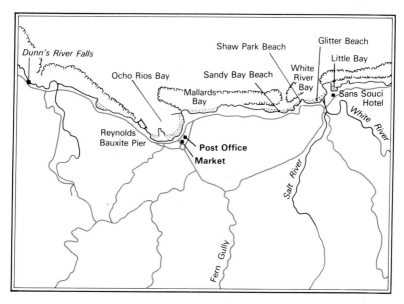

Ocho Rios

The township is not built around a central square or large business area. It flows along both sides of the highway from the Reynolds Bauxite port to the west to Sans Souci Hotel in the direction of the White River. Houses, shops and booths, cars, pedestrians in shorts, swimming trunks, bikinis, a wild assortment of hats and bikes, generate a holiday feeling. There are two constellations of shops along this pulsing artery, the Ocean Village Shopping Centre and, farther to the east, the Pineapple Shopping Centre.

The Dunns River Falls

Excursions and tours

Dunns River Park and Falls are deservedly popular for their natural beauty and for the fun they provide. The Dunns River cascades six hundred feet down a series of limetone terraces and ledges to a wide beach of white sand, so one can mix freshwater and salt, climb the falls or clamber down them from the Park, and swim in a warmer sea. There are booths in the park where woodcarvers and craftsmen display their work for sale.

Dunns River cruise   Sundays and Fridays, 10:00 am and 2:00 pm can be booked through JADCO.

Dunns River feast   Thursdays, 7:30 pm; steel band, calypso, open bar, barbecue featuring roast suckling pig, chicken, rice-and-peas, plantain, other local specialties. Check with hotel about possibility of rebates for those on half-board or full-board.

Fern Gully and Shaw Park Gardens   These can be taken separately, or together.

Shaw Park Gardens   A quarter of a mile from the roundabout at Ocho Rios, where road to Moneague and Kingston branches off from the north-coast highway; a sign-post indicates side-road to the Gardens; they command extensive view of the coast and Ocho Rios Bay; beautifully landscaped; the site of Old Shaw Park hotel, predecessor of Shaw Park Beach Hotel.

Fern Gully   Return to the Ocho Rios-Kingston road, continue to the entrance to Fern Gully. The road twists and turns, climbing for three miles up a gorge carved out by run-off water, beneath canopy of trees that filter the sunlight and give shelter to tree-ferns and many other varieties of ferns, including delicate maiden-hair. Jamaica has more than five hundred species of ferns. Fern lovers will find an excellent collection in the Herbarium of the Institute of Jamaica, in Kingston. A number of varieties are easily found in Fern Gully, in the Shaw Park Gardens, and along St Ann country roads. A Jamaica variety, the Sword Fern, was taken to America in 1793. Forty years later a new variety suddenly appeared in a greenhouse near Boston; since then the Boston fern has given rise to more than two hundred different forms.

Fern Gully

St Ann's Bay and New Seville   St Ann's Bay, capital of the parish of St Ann, is near to the site of the first Spanish settlement in Jamaica, at New Seville. A statue to Christopher Columbus stands in the yard of the Catholic Church, to the west of the town. Two names associated with St Ann's Bay symbolise the two Jamaicas of earlier years. One is Marcus Garvey, who worked here in a printer's shop as a boy. The other was an Anglican priest, The Revd William Bridges, a strong upholder of slavery and opponent of the Dissenters like William Knibb and the emancipationists. Tragedy lived with him. His wife celebrated the year of emanication, 1834, by emancipating herself. She slipped away on to a sloop bound for England. Three years later, while a guest on board a ship in the harbour, Bridges watched the ship's boat capsize just byond the reef and his four young daughters and some òf their friends drown. He became a recluse and later went off to Canada with his son, who later entered the British navy. Bridges eventually became a country curate in England.

Sevilla la Nueva   First Spanish settlement in Jamaica, and one of the earliest in the Americas, was founded in 1510, at the point where Columbus made his first landing. The Columbus monument, referred to above, is the work of an Italian, Michele Guerisi, Jr, and was cast in the explorer's native city, Genoa. Columbus spent more time in Jamaica than anywhere else in the Americas, though not of his wish. He was marooned with his crew near St Ann's Bay for a year (1504). The Arawaks, at first friendly, became hostile, and refused to supply the Spaniards with food. Knowing that an eclipse was due, Columbus told them his god would show his anger by blotting out the moon. When the eclipse took place the terrified Indians agreed to continue supplying the Admiral and his men with food.

New Seville never flourished. The site was unhealthy, and the Spaniards moved their capital to Spanish Town. The ruins of some of the Spanish buildings remain. Excavations have revealed parts of a castle, and a gun position. Parts of a sculptured stone frieze found on the site are now at the Institute of Jamaica. Restoration work is in process.

Green Grotto Caves or **Runaway Caves**   Open daily, 9:00 am to 5:30 pm; 20 miles west of Ocho Rios and 1½ miles east of Runaway Bay; large caves, easily reached; guided tour with lighted pathways includes boat trip on a large underground lake. There is a large lagoon near the caves, up to 170 feet deep.

Prospect Plantation   Tours by open jitney 10:30 am and 3:30 pm, weekdays, 11:00 am and 3:00 pm Sundays; well-managed property offers insight into cultivation of bananas, sugar-cane, coconuts, and making of copra. Splendid view of north coast and, on fair days, Cuba's mountain range from Sir Harold's Viewpoint. Wednesdays, 11:00 am to 1:00 pm Jamaica planta-

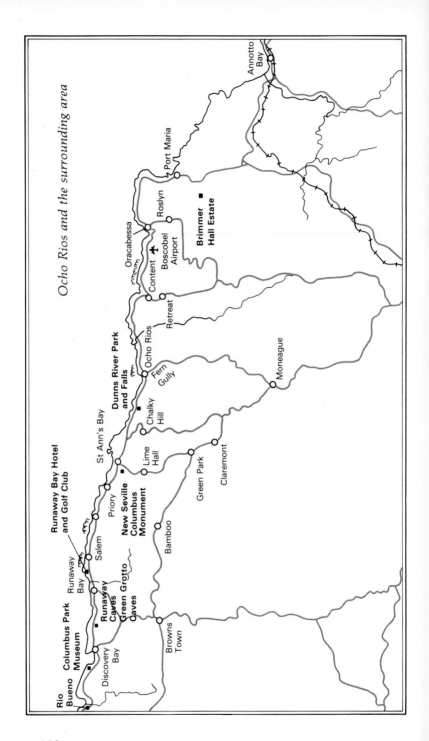

Ocho Rios and the surrounding area

Annotto Bay

Port Maria

Roslyn

Brimmer Hall Estate

Oracabessa

Content

Boscobel Airport

Retreat

Ocho Rios

Dunns River Park and Falls

Fern Gully

Moneague

St Ann's Bay

Chalky Hill

Lime Hall

Green Park

Claremont

Priory

New Seville Columbus Monument

Salem

Bamboo

Runaway Bay Hotel and Golf Club

Runaway Bay

Runaway Caves

Green Grotto Caves

Browns Town

Columbus Park Museum

Discovery Bay

Rio Bueno

tion lunch, codfish and ackee, mackerel and green banana, breadfruit, coffee; music, story-telling. Possible arrangement of horseback tours through White River gorge, or around plantation.

Silver Spray Club, Runaway Bay (tel: 973-3413) Open house on Friday afternoons to see collection of furniture, early American prints and paintings in the home of retired US Naval Commander Jordan L Mott.

Brimmer Hall Estate Take the north coast road from Ocho Rios by way of Couples Hotel (3½ miles), across the Rio Nuevo (5.9 miles) where the English defeated Yssassi, by way of the Golden Head Hotel, through Oracabessa seaport, passing Golden Eye, home of the late Ian Fleming; to Port Maria, nineteen miles. Continue beyond the General Hospital, then turn right on to road to Baileys Vale and Brimmer Hall, two miles away. The estate organises tractor-drawn jitney tours three times daily of 700-acre banana and coconut estate; Great House closed to visitors but bar and swimming pool available. Eating House with Jamaican dishes for lunch; well-stocked souvenir shop; local carvings, paintings on sale.

Runaway Bay This has become an attractive resort, with well-appointed hotels, excellent sea-bathing, tennis, golf, horseback riding; inland are pimento and cattle properties and smallholdings.

Eaton Hall Great House (tel: 973-3503) A plantation house, remodelled and enlarged, with rooms and suites opening on to gardens and the sea; a four-bedroom villa on a grey limestone ledge above the water. Dining room, lounge and terrace; tennis; access to golf course.

Runaway Bay Hotel and Golf Club (tel; 973-3455) This has a lobby, with 2-storey wings extending through shady gardens to sea; rooms air-conditioned; with balconies; pool and beach; tennis, volley ball; golf course; baby-sitting; scuba-diving instruction; night club with limbo and calypso; lunch, informal, on patio; dinner specialties include roast sirloin, lobster, roast pork Jamaica-style.

Caribbean Isle Inn (tel: 973-2364) A small inn, fourteen rooms; pool; clean, friendly, reasonable rates; has small beach but within walking distance; Cardiff Hall beach; meals include full breakfast, sandwich style lunch, steak and lobster.

Discovery Bay – Columbus Park Museum   Interesting cultural 'mix' of exhibits, including a canoe dug out of a huge silk-cotton tree after the style of the Arawaks; a Spanish water-cooler; a water-wheel used on sugar estates a century ago to supply power; the making of logwood dye, a source of wealth before synthetic dyes came on the market; khus-khus, made from the root of a grass that bears the name.

Rio Bueno – Joe James Gallery, Lobster Bowl Restaurant   (tel: 953-2392)   Rio Bueno, on the coast road from Montego Bay to Ocho Rios, thirty miles from each, gets much less attention than it merits, largely because it has no sandy beaches. This may have been the horseshoe-shaped bay where Columbus first landed in Jamaica, and which he called Puerto Bueno. The port came to life in the last century, its wharf busy with the bustle of loading sugar and rum. Houses and shops of stone lined the street. At the entrance to the village are the ruins of Fort Dundas. One of the stones by the front gateway bears the date 1778. Near the fort, in a walled churchyard, is a small, beautifully proportioned Anglican church, St Marks. Inside the church is a colour print of Rio Bueno as the artist, Joseph Kidd, saw it in the 1830's.

A side-road, unpaved after the first mile, leads from Rio Bueno to Bryan Castle, three miles inland, residence of the greatest historian of the Caribbean during the colonial period, Bryan Edwards. His *History, Civil and Commercial of the West Indian Colonies* (1793) went into five editions and was translated into French and German. The work is much sought after by book-collectors.

Joe James, an English artist who has adoped Jamaica, built his home and gallery here. He supervises an art centre that produces sculpture and wood-carvings. Joe James' work includes sketches, oil paintings and carvings. Meals are served in the Lobster Bowl Restaurant, either inside or on a patio by the water: specialties include lobster, fish, steak, turtle steak.

Discovery Bay ruins

Hotels and guest houses: Ocho Rios and surroundings

Americana Ocho Rios   Box 100, Ocho Rios: (809)-974-2151/9,
(telex 7401 MG-OCHO JA)   **(A)**
325 rooms, 554 beds: single $100–$115; double $50–$57.50 EP;
private bath/shower; air-conditioning; pool; fishing; golf; 10% added
for gratuities; night club/discotheque; beauty parlour; tennis; horseback riding; water sports; located on east side of the semicircular
Ocho Rios harbour.

Hibiscus Lodge Hotel   Box 52, Ocho Rios: (809)-974-2676   **(C)**
19 rooms, 37 beds: single $45.80; double $28.40 EP; private bath/
shower; private beach; 10% added for gratuities; in three acres of
garden; small beach but within easy reach of larger beach; help
available for child care.

Inn on the Beach   Box 342, Ocho Rios: (809)-974-2782/4   **(C)**
46 rooms, 92 beds: single $55, double $30 EP; private bath/shower;
air-conditioning; beach rights; 10% added for gratuities; tour desk.

Jamaica Hilton   Box 51, Ocho Rios: (809)-972-2383/2300,
(cable Hiltels Jamaica).   **(A)**
265 rooms, 451 beds: single $104–$129 EP, $136–$161 MAP; double
$55–$67.50 EP; $87–$99.50 MAP; private bath/shower; air-
conditioning; pool; fishing; golf; private beach; 10% added for
gratuities; night club/discotheque; orchestra; resort shops; beauty
parlour; horseback riding; water sports; on sea front 3 miles west of
Ocho Rios in 22 acres of landscaped grounds; aquatic club for
teaching and excursions.

Jamaica Inn   Box 1, Ocho Rios: (809)-974-2514   **(A)**
45 rooms, 90 beds: single $170; double $107.50–$180 AP; private
bath/shower; air-conditioning; pool; fishing; golf; private beach;
10% added for gratuities; orchestra; horseback riding; long low
building near beach; golf at Upton Country Club.

Ocho Rios Sheraton   Box 245, Ocho Rios: (809)-974-2201,
(telex 7403 SH OCHO JA)   **(A)**
370 rooms, 495 beds: single $96–$110; double $50.50–$57.50 EP;
private bath/shower; air-conditioning; pool; fishing; beach rights;
10% added for gratuities; orchestra; resort shops; beauty parlour;
tennis; horseback riding; water sports.

Plantation Inn   Box 2, Ocho Rios: (809)-974-2501   **(B)**
61 rooms, 120 beds: single $150–$210; double $100–$137.50 MAP;
private bath/shower; air-conditioning; pool; fishing; private beach;
10% added for gratuities; orchestra; resort shops; beauty parlour;
tennis; water sports; set in gardens above beach; golf at Upton
Country Club.

Sans Souci   Box 103, Ocho Rios: (809)-974-2353,
(telex 7403 MG-OCHO JA)   **(A)**
67 rooms, 120 beds: single $140–$180; double $75–$95 EP; private

154

bath/shower; air-conditioning; pool; golf; private beach; 10% added for gratuities; orchestra; beauty parlour; tennis; tropical style villas in garden terraces, with central building; elevator down to lower beach front swimming pool; golf at Upton Country Club. The **Spa** is one of the most efficacious in Jamaica, and is a special attraction.

Shaw Park Beach Hotel   Box 17, Ocho Rios: (809)-974-2552/4, (telex 7405)   (A)
118 rooms, 236 beds: single $142–$152; double $77–$81.50 EP; private bath/shower; air-conditioning; pool; fishing; private beach; 10% added for gratuities; night club/discotheque; orchestra; resort shops; beauty parlour; water sports; tour desk; on Cutlass Bay; golf at Upton Country Club.

Silver Sands   Box 81, Ocho Rios: (809)-974-2755/5005   (B)
83 rooms, 160 beds; single $70; double $40 EP; private bath/shower; air-conditioning; pool; fishing; private beach; 10% added for gratuities; night club/discotheque; tennis; water sports; tour desk.

Turtle Beach Apartment   Box 73, Ocho Rios: (809)-974-2801-5   (B)
125 rooms, 246 beds; single $80–$90; double $44–$53.50 EP; private bath/shower; air-conditioning; pool; fishing; 10% added for gratuities; tennis; water sports. Located on Ocho Rios Bay; high rise building.

Hotels and guest houses: toward Port Maria

Couples   Tower Isle PO, St Mary: (809)-974-4271-5   (A)
139 rooms, 278 beds: $135 AP; private bath/shower; air-conditioning; pool; private beach; beach rights; night club/discotheque; resort shops; beauty parlour; tennis; horseback riding; water sports. Wide curving beach with tiny offshore island; only couples accepted for registration; initial fee covers use of all facilities; three meals a day; drinks. The hotel is 3.6 miles east of Ocho Rios on main road to Port Maria.

Casa Maria   Box 10, Port Maria PO: (809)-994-2323-4   (C)
30 rooms, 70 beds: single $30 EP, $38 MAP; double $20 EP, $35 MAP; private bath/shower; partial air-conditioning; cottages; private beach; 10% added for gratuities; resort shops; beauty parlour; tennis.

Hotels and guest houses: Runaway Bay

(43 miles east of Montego Bay, 17 miles west of Ocho Rios)
Berkley Beach   Box 20, Runaway Bay: (809)-973-2066   (C)
76 rooms, 152 beds: single $80; double $45 EP; private bath/shower; air-conditioning; pool; fishing; golf; private beach; 10% added for

gratuities; night club/discotheque; orchestra; resort shops; beauty parlour; tennis; water sports.

Caribbean Isle   Box 119, Runaway Bay; (809)-973-2364   **(C)**
14 rooms, 28 beds: single $30; double $22.50 EP; private bath/shower; air-conditioning; pool; beach rights; 10% added for gratuities; night club/discotheque.

Club Caribbean   Box 65, Runaway Bay: (809)-973-3507-9   **(B)**
116 rooms, 232 beds: single $90–$101; double $61–$67 MAP; private bath/shower; partial air-conditioning; pool; cottages; golf; private beach; night club/discotheque; orchestra; resort shops; beauty parlour; tennis; horseback riding; water sports.

Eaton Hall Great House   Box 112, Runaway Bay:
(809)-973-3507/9   **(A)**
56 rooms, 108 beds: single $119–$179 AP, double $99–$120 AP; private bath/shower; air-conditioning; pool; cottages; beach rights; 10% added for gratuities; tennis; tour desk. The brick foundation may be that of an old fort dating back to the late 17th century. The hotel is within walking distance of the Cardiff Hall Beach and an 18-hole golf club.

Runaway Bay   Box 58, Runaway Bay: (809)-973-3435/7,
(telex 7409 RUNBAHTL, JA)   **(B)**
152 rooms, 254 beds: rates on application; private bath/shower; air-conditioning; pool; fishing; golf; private beach; 10% added for gratuities; night club/discotheque; orchestra; resort shops; beauty parlour; tennis; horseback riding; water sports; tour desk.

Silver Spray   Box 16, Runaway Bay: (809)-973-3413   **(C)**
19 rooms, 38 beds: single $50–$75 EP, $75–$100 MAP; double $57.50–$62.50 EP, $50 MAP; private bath/shower; air-conditioning; pool; fishing; golf; private beach; 10% added for gratuities; tennis; water sports.

156

12 Port Antonio, the Rio Grande and Bath Spa

General information

Port Antonio, capital of the parish of Portland, is on the north-east coast of Jamaica, almost at the point where the coast swings sharply south. It has a population of 10 000, about one-tenth that of the whole parish.

By air Port Antonio is seventeen minutes from the Tinson Pen airport in Kingston. As the crow flies it is twenty-two miles away but the Blue Mountain range intervenes, so travellers by road have to go around or over the barrier. One road follows the coast by way of Manchioneal and Hectors River to Holland Estate where it turns west toward Kingston by way of Morant Bay. The distance is seventy-seven miles, the time 2½ hours.

The other popular route is by the A4 west to Annotto Bay, and then by the A3, which follows the valley of the Wag Water, bobbing and weaving for some twenty miles until it comes into open country; then by way of Stony Hill to Kingston. This is a shorter route, sixty miles, and the road is well-surfaced, but the corkscrew stretch in the middle section calls for caution.

A third route follows the A4 to Buff Bay, then turns left on to the B1, and climbs up to Hardwar Gap, 4000 feet high. Having passed through the Gap, it descends by way of Newcastle to Papine and Kingston. The distance is sixty miles, but much of the twenty-three miles between Buff Bay and Hardwar Gap is rough going. Visitors who use this road or who drive up any of the Portland valleys soon see how mountainous a parish Portland is. Two-thirds of it, 240 square miles, is more than 1000 feet above sea level; one third is more than 3000 feet high.

157

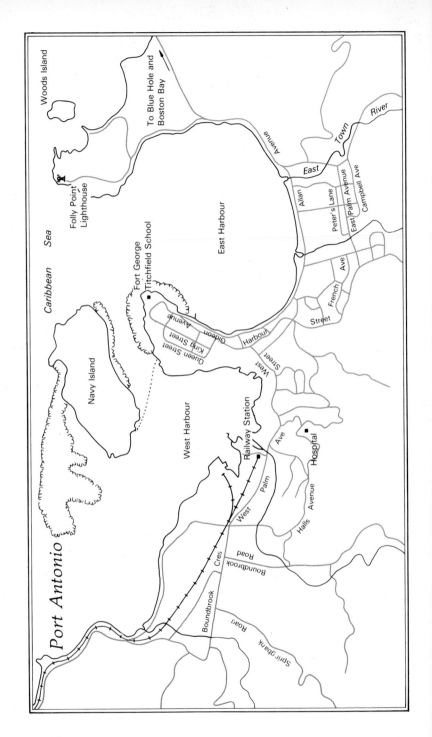

Port Antonio

As a result, Portland is less densely populated than most Jamaican parishes. Also, it was never a sugar parish. The chief products are bananas and coconuts, with some cattle. The mountain slopes face the north-east trade winds, which sweep in heavy with rainclouds making the high mountains and valleys the wettest part of Jamaica, feeding streams and tributaries into the Rio Grande, the Swift River, the Buff Bay River and other Portland rivers. It is drier along the coast. Port Antonio has an average of twenty-four sunny days a month. When the rain comes it falls heavily, then it clears and the sun returns.

Superlatives are always suspect, but Port Antonio's twin harbours deserve them. They are best seen from a vantage point such as the Bonnie View Hotel. The road up climbs sharply but is quite safe. From the hotel grounds it is possible to pick out Upper Titchfield on a narrow promontory that separates East Harbour from West Harbour; the old military barracks of Fort George and the Titchfield School; Navy Island, a mini-edition of Crusoe's island, covered with coconut trees; and Lower Titchfield which runs west along the waterfront, with wharves, shops, Town Hall and market. The deep blue of the West Harbour in its emerald setting of palms, the unspoiled perfection of Navy Island guarding the channel and providing the eye with a near horizon, and the sea-green of the shallower East Harbour make this one of the loveliest harbours to be found anywhere.

Mystery and grandeur are the words for Port Antonio and its surroundings, in spite of the fact that parts of the town are shabby and down-at-heels; that the galvanised tin roofs of some of the shops and houses are rusty; and that the streets of the town are mean in their proportions. The natural beauty gives a charm even to these; and mystery and grandeur remain the words.

The mountains set the mood. Portlanders are mountain-loving people, though steep hillsides break the back of a farmer. 'To reach my district,' said a Portland woman, 'you have to travel five miles of continuous hill with the houses jotted in between.' She was one of the Maroon people who live around Moore Town. Their story adds to the mystery of the mountains. To this day they are credited with special skills in

Port Antonio

folk-medicine, in the use of healing leaves to make 'Maroon blister'; and there are stories of how they used vines and withes, 'Maroon wiss-wiss' to camouflage themselves, and of how they used sharp-pointed wooden lances, 'maroon lance' in fighting and hunting.

As a child born in a Methodist manse near Manchioneal, I still recall the excitement and fear with which I listened to 'Cookie' as she told stories about the Maroons, how they

hunted wild pigs in the mountains and cooked 'jerk pork'; how they could find their way through the John Crow mountains; how they talked to each other on the abeng or bull horn; how they had the power of appearing and disappearing. She told also how Nanny, one of the Maroon leaders, held out against the English soldiers; how she could heal those Maroons who were wounded; how she absorbed the bullets of the English soldiers in her capacious backside. She told how, at Nanny

Town now, white birds roost in the trees at evening time, birds such as no one ever sees by day, for they are the ghosts of the Nanny Town dead.

Portland offers beauty that is at times almost overwhelming. Those who discover it usually return. It also offers a challenge. To get to know the land and its people one needs to go into the valleys of the Rio Grande and Swift River, to visit Millbank and Moore Town, Golden Vale, Skibo, Coopers Hill and the upper reaches of the Back River. Guides are available for those who wish to go into less frequented country.

This combination of natural beauty and challenge, of mystery and grandeur, captivated Errol Flynn. He fell in love with Portland, bought Navy Island and Comfort Castle Estate, where his widow Patrice Wymore still lives, and popularised rafting on the Rio Grande. The older people who knew him loved him. 'He was a kind man,' they will tell you.

Tours and excursions

The Rio Grande and Moore Town   Rafting starts at Berridale, but it is well worth driving first to Moore Town. The Road leads from Port Antonio through Fellowship (4 miles), Golden Vale, and then along a high cliff overlooking the river. Pause to wonder at the glory of Blue Mountain Peak, and then proceed to Moore Town. To the east are the John Crow Mountains. They have an average height of just over 2000 feet, but they have rarely been crossed because the higher part is a waterless plateau of sharp honeycomb limestone. The range divides the Rio Grande valley from the east coast.

Moore Town, named after Governor Henry Moore (1760–62), is on the banks of the Rio Grande. It was settled by the Maroons who, as has been noted, waged a long guerilla war against the British in the 18th century. Those who wish to visit Moore Town should seek the help of the Tourist Board office in Port Antonio, so that their leader, the Colonel, can be notified in advance. The great festival of the year at Moore Town is the celebration in honour of Nanny, who is a national hero; the abeng horns, coromantee drums and dances fill the day with sound, and the old stories and legends are retold.

Having visited Moore Town it is worth returning to Berridale to embark on a rafting expedition. The raft is of bamboo, twenty-three feet wide, thirty-three feet long, sturdy, with a raised seat for two toward the back. The river captain stands at the front using a long pole to guide the raft through rapids and quiet stretches, passing banana plantations, coconut trees, through the Tunnel of Love – a narrow passage between high cliffs – for eight miles to the Rafter's Rest at Burlington on St Margaret's Bay.

On this trip of half-a-day it is noticeable that there are no Great Houses, no sugar factories, no spreading fields of sugar-cane, no plantations, just patches and fields of bananas and other food crops. This is the country of the Portland small-holders who gave Jamaica its banana industry, growing on their patches of land the bananas that Captain Baker and his successors bought and took to the United States.

Fishing and scenic tours

Port Antonio is a popular centre for deep-sea fishing. Large marlin have been taken: wahoo, tarpon, snook, snapper, jack fish and barracuda. In the higher waters of the Rio Grande, Swift and Spanish rivers there are mountain mullet, Hognose mullet and drummer. Those keen on fresh-water and deep-sea fishing should consult with the Jamaica Tourist Board.

Blue Lagoon or Blue Hole   Seven miles from Port Antonio on A3 coast road. Signs point the way from the main road down to the beach, to a restaurant and bar overlooking the lagoon, a large circular expanse of startlingly blue water, 180 feet deep. Visitors are admitted between 10 am and 10 pm daily. Facilities include waterskiing in the bay, scuba-diving off the reef, trips in a glass-bottomed boat, rental of waterskiing and diving equipment. On leaving, if the light allows, continue a short way along the A3 east, then stop and look down on the lagoon, intensely blue in a setting of dark-green trees.

The restaurant, which looks out on the beach, serves seafood, and on Sundays there is a barbecue. Drinks are available. In the winter season a calypso band plays nightly, and at weekends at other times.

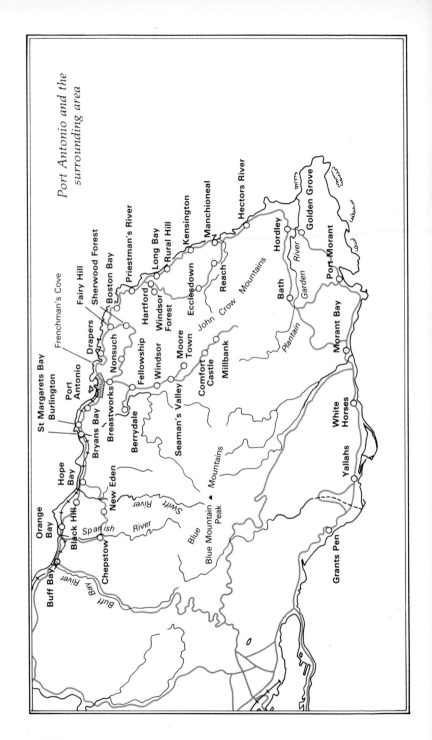

Port Antonio and the surrounding area

Boston Beach Ten miles east of Port Antonio, it is protected by an off-shore reef. It has an excellent beach of fine sand, and is ideal for a swim and picnic.

Scenic Tours include:

(a) going from **Port Antonio** to **Swift River**, and **Mount Hermon** to **Chepstow**, through **Skibo** and back by way of **Black Hill**;

(b) by way of the **Park Mountain** road and **Golden Vale** for a magic combination of river and mountain scenery;

(c) **Somerset Falls,** ten miles west of Port Antonio, past Hope Bay on the A4. The Daniels River plunges down a narrow gorge bordered with tropical rainforests. There are picnic places and bathing in cool, deep rock pools;

(d) The **Caves of Nonsuch** and the **Gardens of Athenry,** beyond the **Blue Lagoon.** The signs point right, away from the A3. This side road leads for six miles through small villages, to the Caves and the Gardens. It is possible to continue along the road which twists and turns back to Port Antonio;

(e) **Camera Safaris** set out every Thursday at 11 am from the Burlington House near Rafter's Rest, for a 2½ hour horseback ride into the Blue Mountains and along the Rio Grande.

The East Coast and Bath Spa Take the A3 east, past San San Bay, Frenchman's Cove, the Blue Lagoon (7 miles) and Boston Beach (10 miles). The coastal plain is much narrower, for the sombre John Crow Mountains press down on the coast, leaving little elbow-room.

Gradually the vegetation and the aspect of the land changes from lush tropical to arid and windswept. From Priestman's River, we drive along a windy rock-bound coast where the trees lean inland under the pressure of the trade winds; past Long Bay, with its fine beach and lively sea; by way of Manchioneal whose name is a reminder of an early botanist's description of the manchineel tree as 'full of a very fiery and hot milk' with a fruit that turned into worms when eaten; if anyone were to sleep under its shade 'their head swells and they grow blind'. The leaves of the tree contain an irritant.

The Reach Falls, near Manchioneal, are among the most spectacular in the island. Turn off the main road just before the

Driver's River Bridge and proceed with caution – for the road is rough – for two miles to a fork in the road, where an unobtrusive sign points down some steps to the falls and caves. Without doubt the falls will be 'developed' as an attraction but, as they now are, they have an unspoiled charm.

Continue through Manchioneal and along the Ken Jones Highway, named after a young Jamaican legislator who was born at Hectors River and met a tragic death. At Hectors River (50 miles) there is a Quaker's Chapel and a secondary school, started early in the century by American Quakers.

The road leads on to Quao Hill, named after a Maroon Chief; from the summit there is a view of Holland Point, the island's most easterly tip, and of part of a wide fertile plain watered by the Plantain Garden River. Descend the escarpment, and drive through Hordley to Golden Grove, in the middle of the Holland Estate. The mountains recede and the ribbon of the coastal plain broadens out into fields of sugar-cane, coconuts, bananas and pastures for cattle. Though now the south coast, it is not beyond the rain-bearing influence of the trade winds. There is also a change from the smallholder economy and culture of the Blue Mountain valleys into the estate economy and culture based, originally, on sugar.

Holland Estate once belonged to Simon Taylor, who sat in the Jamaica House of Assembly from 1763 to 1810. The richest West Indian planter of his time, he boasted that on his death his nephew Simon would be the richest commoner in England. He hated the Baptist and Methodist missionaries who preached against slavery, insisting that slaves should be treated as human beings. He had a fierce reputation for detesting women, but he fathered a number of children on his various estates.

Lady Nugent, in her diary, tells of the vast meals with which Simon Taylor entertained her husband Governor Nugent and herself. On parting, he said, 'I am very sorry, Ma'am, but good Almighty God, I must go home and cool coppers.' She thought he was referring to some sugar-making process but 'I found he meant he must go home and be abstemious, after so much feasting'. Continue to Bath, thirty-seven miles further on, in Lady Nugent's day 'truly a lovely village at the bottom of an immense mountain'.

166

The Bath Botanical Gardens and the Bath Spa

In the second half of the 18th century the British and French governments recognised the importance of augmenting the food-supply in their Caribbean sugar colonies by introducing new forms of starch. Cook's voyages in the Pacific had also stimulated an interest in botany. Botanical gardens were founded in a number of West Indian islands, such as St Vincent, Dominica and Jamaica. The Bath Gardens are full of a variety of plants, breadfruit, cabbage trees, jack-fruit, cinnamon, the star apple, whose leaf is bronze on one side, bright green on the other side, and the otaheite tree which has a bright pink blossom, like a tassel

The Bath Spa is two miles beyond the town. Lady Nugent, modestly clad in night-cap, dressing gown and pokey bonnet, set off on horseback along the narrow winding path to the spa, which contained four rooms, with a marble bath in each.

Then there is another house for infirm negroes ... they tell
you of wonderful cures performed by the waters ... which
I really found most delightful and refreshing.

The old woman attending the bath was very anxious to see her but her pokey bonnet covered her face and her dressing-gown concealed her person.

Stepping out of the bath in a perfectly undisguised state,
she heard a voice near her and perceived, under the door,
a pair of black eyes, and indeed a whole black face,
looking earnestly at her; for the door was half-a-yard too
short ... and [the old woman] laid herself down on her
stomach to peep.... The Governor's Lady let out a great
squall and away ran the old lady.

The Bath was opened in 1699, after a slave told how the water had cured his ulcerated leg. The Government bought 1300 acres of land around the spring; or perhaps 'springs' would be more accurate since hot radioactive springs and cooler water pour out of the same igneous rocks above Sulphur River. The water is mixed in the Baths to a comfortable bathing temperature. It contains lime and sulphur as well as other minerals, and is of great benefit to persons suffering from skin troubles of various sorts, and from various rheumatic ailments.

Driving west toward Kingston, the names Morante and

Yallahs testify to the period of Spanish settlement when cattle were let loose on the *hato* of Morante and around the salt ponds at Yallahs. The highway by-passes Morant Bay, chief town of the parish of St Thomas, but it would be a pity not to drive through and to stop however briefly at the Court House to look at the memorial to Paul Bogle, which was created by Jamaica's leading sculptor, Edna Manley,

Morant Bay and St Thomas are of special interest to all Jamaicans because of the rising which took place here in 1865, when discontent bred by three years of drought, repressive and unjust laws and an authoritarian Governor, provoked an outbreak. Paul Bogle led a demonstration of peasants from his church in Stony Gut to Morant Bay. Rioting broke out, the Court House was burnt down and the Custos was killed along with a number of white planters who were in the Court House. Disturbances broke out in other parts of the parish. The Governor, Eyre, called out the troops and the rising was put down with great cruelty, four hundred and fifty people being executed, six hundred flogged and more than a thousand buildings destroyed. Paul Bogle was hanged. George William

A stamp commemorating the centenary of the Morant Bay Rebellion

Gordon was taken from Kingston to Morant Bay and hanged, for the Governor considered he had fomented the rebellion because he had championed the cause of the peasants and was a friend of Bogle's. The statue to Bogle stands in front of the Court House. Behind it, looking out to the harbour, is a memorial to those who died for their part in the rising.

The Morant Bay rising marked a turning point in Jamaica's history, because it resulted in the surrender by the House of Assembly of the old representative system of government and in the institution of Crown Colony rule. St Thomas influenced the island's cultural development because it became the home, after the emancipation of the slaves in 1833, of a number of free Africans who were imported as contract workers. They brought with them their *cumina* cult and dances, and these fed strength into indigenous art forms. From earlier plantation times the legend of Three-Finger Jack was preserved; a black Robin Hood, who frequented the lonely hills around Bull Bay and White Horses, robbing and plundering, but never molesting the poor.

Leaving Morant Bay for Kingston, pass over the Bustamante Bridge, one of the longest in Jamaica, and continue by way of Rozelle, a pleasant picnic spot, Yallahs, Grants Pen and Bull Bay. The arid fields and eroded hills are in sharp contrast to the green cane-fields and luxuriant foliage of eastern St Thomas. You have passed into the shadow of the mountains, which bar the rain-bearing north-east trade winds.

Hotels and guest houses: Port Antonio

Bonnie View Box 82, Port Antonio: (809)-993-2752   (C)
30 rooms, 60 beds: single $30; double $25 EP; private bath/shower; partial air-conditioning; pool; cottages; beach rights; 10% added for gratuities; tennis; 600 feet above sea-level; overlooking harbour; back garden looks up to Blue Mountain Peak; free seats in staff bus into and from Port Antonio.
Dragon Bay Box 176, Port Antonio: (809)-993-3281-3   (A)
99 rooms, 165 beds: rates on application; private bath/shower; air-conditioning; pool; cottages; private beach; beach rights; 15% added for gratuities; night club/discotheque; resort shops; tennis; water sports. All chalets set in extensive grounds, self-contained, around private bay.

Jamaica Hill   Box 26, Port Antonio: (809)-993-3286/7   **(A)**
44 rooms, 88 beds: rates on application; private bath/shower; air-conditioning; pool; cottages; private beach; beach rights; 10% added for gratuities; tennis; horseback riding. Located on hill overlooking Princess Island; 44 villas in extensive grounds.

Trident Villas   Box 119, Port Antonio: (809)-993-2602/2705   **(A)**
28 rooms, 56 beds: single $198–$238; double $125–$145 MAP; private bath/shower; pool; cottages; fishing; private beach; resort shops; beauty parlour; tennis; horseback riding; water sports. Villas set in gardens; large bedrooms; private patios; formal dinner.

Restaurants

Stage Door Restaurant   City Centre Plaza, upstairs, next door to Jamaica Tourist Board Office; Jamaican cuisine, including beef soup, steak, baked chicken, curried goat, tripe and red beans, sweet potato pie.

Blue Lagoon Restaurant   beside the Lagoon, 5 miles east of Port Antonio; Jamaican dishes include lobster salad, fricassée chicken, fish, and vegetarian meals; Sundays, barbecue from 11 am to 5 pm.

Boston Bay Beach has a jerk-pork barbecue, highly spiced.

13 Kingston, Port Royal, Spanish Town and the Blue Mountains

General information

Could one design a more perfect stage-setting, one more full of theatre, of drama?

In the background is the Blue Mountain range, reaching up to the sky. In the dawn, the highest peaks are set afire by the rising sun, and at evening they are soft lilac. In the middle distance are the Port Royal mountains, with vertical valleys like the sculptured folds of a Greek carving; and land that slides gently from six hundred feet to sea-level. In the foreground there are twenty-five square miles of water almost encircled by a thin protecting strip of land. At dawn the enclosed water is pigeon grey and the outer sea restless celadon green.

Kingston grew out of the ashes of disaster. Today it is the capital of Jamaica, the island's chief commercial centre, and the largest city in the Commonwealth Carribbean. Its buildings cover an area of more than twenty-five square miles and its suburbs climb up Long Mountain, Jacks Hill, Stony Hill and the Red Hills. In 1690 none of this existed. At the harbour's edge there were some fishermen's huts. The great centre of trade was Port Royal, across the harbour. The island's capital was Spanish Town, which had been founded by the Spanish colonists. In 1692 an earthquake destroyed Port Royal, and some merchants moved to Kingston. They lived there in huts made with boughs, while others remained in Port Royal and attempted to make a fresh start. Two or three fires frustrated their efforts, and they also moved across the harbour.

The names of some of the city streets go back to this early

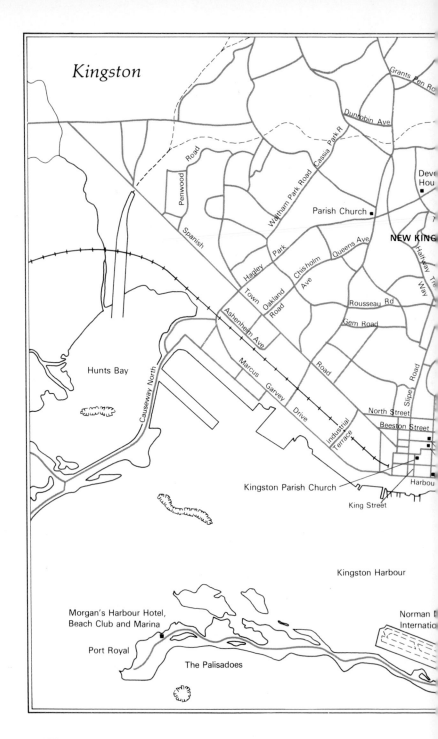

Kingston

Grants Pen Rd

Dunrobin Ave

Penwood Road

Spanish

Waltham Park Road

Cassia Park R

Parish Church

Dev
Hou

NEW KING

Hagley
Park

Chisholm
Ave

Queens Ave

Halfway Tre
Way

Town

Oakland
Road

Rousseau Rd

Gem Road

Ashenheim Ave

Hunts Bay

Causeway North

Marcus

Garvey

Drive

Road

Industrial
Terrace

Slipe Road

North Street

Beeston Street

Harbou

Kingston Parish Church

King Street

Kingston Harbour

Morgan's Harbour Hotel,
Beach Club and Marina

Norman
Internatio

Port Royal

The Palisadoes

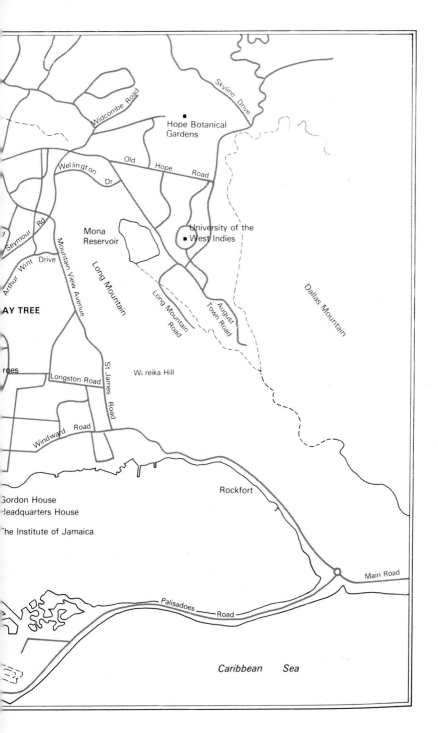

Widcombe Road

Skyline Drive

Hope Botanical
Gardens

Wellington

Dr

Old

Hope

Road

Seymour Rd

Mona
Reservoir

University of the
West Indies

Arthur Wint Drive

Mountain View Avenue

Long Mountain

Dallas Mountain

AY TREE

Long Mountain Road

August Town Road

roes

St. James Road

Longston Road

W: reika Hill

Windward Road

Rockfort

Gordon House
Headquarters House

The Institute of Jamaica

Main Road

Palisadoes

Road

Caribbean   Sea

period. Port Royal Street reminds us of the Port Royal merchants to whom land was allotted on the waterfront. Barry Street is named after Colonel Samuel Barry, who first owned the land; Beeston Street is named after William Beeston, Governor of the island at the end of the century who bought the land from Barry. North, East and West Streets mark the limits of the old city, which was in the shape of a grid-iron, with an open space in the centre, the Parade, now the Parade Gardens.

Port Royal, commanding the entrance to the harbour, grew in importance as a naval base, while Kingston became by 1703 the island's chief port of entry and commercial centre. In 1872

Kingston at twilight

the seat of government was moved from Spanish Town to Kingston.

In 1907 the city, which had survived a number of fires and hurricanes, was severely damaged by an earthquake and by fire. The city was rebuilt and expanded rapidly, outgrowing its old system of administration based on a small municipality; so in 1923 parts of the parish of St Andrew were merged with Kingston to form the Corporation of Kingston and St Andrew, administered by a Mayor and Corporation.

Commercial Kingston also outgrew its former limits, and New Kingston was developed to accommodate hotels, banks,

commercial offices and a shopping plaza. An industrial estate was laid out in west Kingston, and a modern deep-water harbour was created at Newport West, with a free port and facilities for transhipment. Low and middle income housing estates were built, and satellite towns were established, such as Havendale and Independence City.

The Kingston waterfront has been transformed. A foreshore road spans Hunts Bay and brings Port Henderson within ten minutes of Kingston. There are ghettos and squalid slums in parts of west and eastern Kingston, but impressive progress has been made in creating a capital city worthy of its incomparable setting. For an up-to-date list of Kingston hotels, restaurants and guest houses, please apply to the Jamaica Tourist Board, 79–81 Knutsford Blvd., Kingston 5.

Places of interest

Downtown The Institute of Jamaica; The Bank of Jamaica's Coin and Note Museum; Kingston Parish Church; Craft Market; Headquarters House and Gordon House; Heroes Park; The National Gallery of Jamaica; The Cultural Centre.

Midtown and New Kingston Devon House

Mona The Hope Botanical Gardens; the University of the West Indies.

Downtown: The Institute of Jamaica, 12 East Street, Kingston. This is a treasure house, near the waterfront, with a Natural History Museum, History Gallery, and a National Library, formerly the West India Reference Library. Founded in 1879 'for the encouragement of literature, science and art', it houses Jamaica's great cultural heritage, with a remarkable collection of maps, prints, documents and books relating to Jamaica and the West Indies. Its herbarium contains many specimens of Jamaican and West Indian plants, with a first-class section of Jamaican ferns; and it has a comprehensive collection of Jamaican butterflies as well as of other insects. Cultural activities include exhibitions of work by Jamaican artists.

The building stands on the site of a popular boarding house,

The headquarters of the Law of the Seabed Authority, Kingston

Date Tree Hall, of the 1850s. This is associated with the name of Mary Seacole, whose portrait hangs in the gallery. She gained a great reputation as a nurse in a terrible cholera epidemic of 1850 in Jamaica; later, in Central America, she was known as 'the yellow woman from Jamaica with the cholera medicine'. In 1854, after the Crimean war between Britain and France broke out, Mary Seacole made her way to the Crimea, met Florence Nightingale, established herself in a rough wooden building near Balaclava which she called the British Hotel, and got on with the job of nursing and feeding the soldiers who called her 'Mother Seacole'. Queen Victoria decorated her with two medals for her services to the troops. There is on display in the Museum a small terracotta bust of her by Count Gleichen, a nephew of Queen Victoria.

The 'Shark Papers' are among the Institute's most famous exhibits. In 1799, while Britain and France were at war, a British frigate, HMS *Sparrow*, patrolling off the coast of Haiti, sighted a brig with a damaged mast, boarded her and sent her as a prize of war to Port Royal, for trial in the Court of Vice-Admiralty. The German owners of the brig, the *Nancy*, and the master contested the case and produced papers that seemed satisfactory. The *Sparrow*, under Commander Wylie, continued its patrol off the south coast of Haiti, in company with a small tender, the *Ferret*, commanded by Lieutenant Fitton. Some sailors on the *Ferret* caught a shark, pulled it aboard, cut it up, and found in its stomach a bundle of papers. Soon afterwards Wylie, in conversation with Fitton, referred to the trial of the *Nancy* and Fitton said, 'I have her papers'. 'But,' replied Wylie, 'I sealed up those papers and sent them in with her.' 'Those were the false papers,' replied Fitton. 'Here are the real ones.' The shark papers and some found in the captain's cabin in a case of salt meat proved the case against the *Nancy*, which was condemned as a prize of war.

Kingston Crafts Market, at the west end of Harbour Street, consists of a large number of stalls, each individually owned, with displays of carvings, straw goods, pottery, beautifully embroidered cloths, and coloured ceramic figurines of considerable merit.

Kingston Parish Church, at the corner of King Street and South Parade, contains some monuments and tombstones of historic interest, such as the black marble gravestone of Admiral John Benbow, who attacked a French squadron off Cartagena in 1702, and was deserted by two of his captains who were later court-martialled and shot. Benbow had his leg shattered by chain-shot, but he continued to direct the action. He was brought back to Port Royal where he died of his wounds. In the north transept there is a monument to a goldsmith, John Wolmer, whose bequest made possible the founding of Wolmer's School in 1736.

Headquarters House and Gordon House are on Duke Street, across the road from each other. Jamaica's Parliament meets at Gordon House, named in honour of George William Gordon. Of greater interest architecturally is Headquarters House, built about the middle of the 18th century by Thomas Hibbert, a Kingston merchant. The story goes that four rich Kingston merchants made a wager as to who could build the finest mansion, and that Hibbert won.

Heroes Park   Continue north up Duke Street, cross over North Street, which marked the northern limits of the old city, to Heroes Park, which occupies the southern part of the old Kingston Race Course. The Park contains monuments to the builders of modern Jamaica; George William Gordon and Paul Bogle who were executed for their part in the Morant Bay rising, Marcus Garvey, William Alexander Bustamante and Norman Washington Manley.

Further north are two of the longest established educational institutions in Jamaica. Wolmer's School was founded in 1736 through a bequest from a Kingston jeweller, John Wolmer; this was just eighteen years after Elihu Yale's benefaction led to the founding of Yale University.

To the north of Wolmer's is Mico College. The story of its funding begins in 1670, when Barbary pirates were terrorising the Mediterranean, and taking Christians as slaves. In 1670 Lady Mico left £1000 'for the redemption of poor Christian slaves in Barbary'. When there were no longer Christian slaves in Barbary, the pirates having been eliminated by Admiral Blake, the money accumulated, reaching £120000 in 1827. Sir Thomas Fowell Buxton, a friend of Wilberforce and a keen emancipator, prepared a programme, which the British Court of Chancery accepted, for using the money to promote education among the black and coloured population of British Guyana and the West Indies. Mico College was founded in 1838 with money from the Mico Trust. Since then it has trained teachers for service in the elementary schools of Jamaica, as well as for some of the other islands, and its alumni have a distinguished record of public service and of educational work at every level in the island. It is not too much to say that old Miconians and the alumni of the various teacher-training colleges for women, St Josephs, Bethlehem and others, were among the foremost in providing Jamaica with the infra-structure, the idealism and the loyalty that independence demands.

Midtown: Devon House is highly recommended. It was built in 1881 by a Jamaican architect and gold miner. It passed through other hands and, by the gift of another merchant, Percy Lindo, is now the property of the Government of Jamaica. Recently redecorated, it is now one of the finest cultural centres in

The Hope Gardens

Jamaica, elegantly furnished, with shops that display some of the island's finest work in jewellery, fabrics, carvings and straw work. It also has a grog shop and gourmet restaurant and is altogether a delightfully refreshing place.

Mona: The Royal Botanical Gardens at Hope cover 150 acres of the north-east corner of the Liguanea Plain, at the foot of the hills, on part of what used to be the Hope Sugar Estate. Some of the aqueducts survive here and on the grounds of the nearby University of the West Indies. The setting is magnificent: spacious lawns, ornamental gardens and borders of bougainvillaea of many varieties which are ablaze with yellows, purples, reds and whites early in the year, against a background of hills with loftier peaks in the distance. There is a highly prized collection of more than two hundred species of orchids. The people of Kingston frequent the gardens on holidays and at weekends, special attractions being a children's garden, called Coconut Park, a maze and a small zoo, with lions and tigers, monkeys, snakes and crocodiles.

The University of the West Indies founded in 1948, occupies a square mile of land on the Mona Common, once the Hope Sugar Estate; a brick aqueduct survives, which took water from the Hope River to the fields of the estate. The Chapel was built from the stones of a ruined Georgian building on a Trelawny sugar estate, Gayle's Valley. The Master Builders of Jamaica took down the old building and transported the stones to Kingston where the University's architects, Norman and Dawbarn, through their local representative Alick Low, designed the new building and supervised its erection.

The University was founded in 1948 and started with thirty-two students. It is supported by fourteen countries of the Commonwealth Caribbean. It has a campus at St Augustine in Trinidad, another at Cave Hill in Barbados, and offices and programmes in all the other supporting countries. In 1981 it had a total enrolment of 8000 undergraduates and graduate students. It reflects the essential unity of the widely-dispersed independent West Indian nations. Like the University of the South West Pacific, its campus includes a vast expanse of sea.

The University has Schools of Medicine, Agriculture, Engineering and Law, as well as the Humanities and the Natural

The University of the West Indies

and Social Sciences. It also has a region-wide extension programme (called extra-mural).
Port Royal is situated at the end of the Palisades, a natural
breakwater seven miles long. The English fortified the point so
as to command the entrance to the harbour and, within a few
years, many English buccaneers had made this their base for
raids against Spanish America. The city grew rapidly, and
became notorious for its wickedness: it was the Babylon of the
West, a City of Gold, The Wickedest Place in Christendom, a
Gilded Hades where common seamen hung their ears with
heavy gold rings studded with gems, where dagger thrusts were
as common as brawls, and the body of a murdered man would
remain in a dance-room until the dancing was over. The taverns

rang with the exploits of Henry Morgan, who took and sacked Porto Bello, and brought back 300 000 pieces of eight; then 250 000 pieces of eight from burning Maracaibo; and 750 000 pieces from Panama on the Pacific coast. Made Governor of Jamaica in 1682, and ordered by the King to put an end to the attacks on Spain and to buccaneering, Morgan offered his former companions a choice between a grant of land and the end of a rope. His way of life made him an old man at forty-five, 'his eyes yellowish, his belly jutting out a little'. With death near, he turned from his doctors to an African medicine man who poulticed him with urine and plastered him over with clay. This finished him off. He died in 1688.

Four years later, while the Rector of the Parish Church was taking a glass of wormwood with the acting Governor, the earth heaved and shook. 'Be not afeard,' the Governor said, 'it will soon be over.' Within three minutes Port Royal was destroyed. The frigate *Swan* in the careening yard keeled over on to one side, the land sank with quays and warehouses, and a tidal wave swept the *Swan* inland, riding high above the roofs. Running towards Morgans Fort, the Rector saw the earth open and swallow a number of people. He hurried past men and women buried up to their necks, some upside down. A tombstone, now in the yard of the Parish Church, records how a French refugee, Lewis Galdey, was swallowed up in the great earthquake ... 'and by the Providence of God was by another Shock Thrown into the sea ...'

John Pike, a Quaker who survived the earthquake, wrote to his brother saying:

'I lost my wife, my son, a 'prentice, a white maid and six slaves. ... My land ... is all sunk; a good sloop may sail over it as well as over the Point.' The wretched survivors, left without shelter, regarded *'a house that is daubed with mortar and thatched, the eaves hanging down almost to the ground, a pleasant house. ... Here you may see colonels and great men bowing down their bodies to creep into a little hutch.'*

Port Royal remained important as a naval base, however, with ships of the line swinging at anchor off the Dockyard. Horatio Nelson, then a frail-looking young officer, kept watch from his quarterdeck on Fort Charles. A year later he was brought back from a sortie against Nicaragua, near death from yellow fever and dysentery. A black woman, Cuba Cornwallis, nursed him back to health. Cuba, who had been a slave, had been freed by Admiral Cornwallis, whose name she took. Over the entrance to Fort Charles are the arms of Nelson, and the wall bears this inscription: 'In this place dwelt Horatio Nelson. You who tread his footprints remember his glory.'

Along with **Fort Charles** other places of special interest are **St Peter's Church**, where memorial tablets on the wall record the deaths of young midshipmen from yellow fever, cholera and dysentery. The silver plate of the Church is said to have been part of the booty Morgan brought back from Panama. Near to the Fort stands the old Naval Hospital, now an Archaeological Museum, with artefacts from the submerged part of the city. The pioneer in this effort at recreating Port Royal's past was an American, Edward Link, who in 1959 located the sunken walls of houses, and recovered cannon-barrels and domestic items including a brass watch dated 1686 whose hands had stopped at 11:43, the time of the earthquake. The hands had disappeared but X-ray pictures revealed traces of them.

The University of the West Indies maintains a **Marine Biology Research Station** at Port Royal. Visitors interested in learning about the research and teaching programmes should make contact with the Public Relations officer of the University, (tel: (809)-927-9925).

Morgan's Harbour Hotel, Beach Club and Marina, (tel: (809)-938-7223), on the eastern side of Port Royal, can be reached by ferry from Ocean Boulevard, Kingston, or by car or taxi from the Norman Manley International Airport or from Kingston by way of Rockfort. The hotel has a large seafront patio, a marina with boats moored along the jetty, a restaurant and bar, and a swimming area which is roped off from the boating area. From the patio there is a view across the harbour to Kingston and the mountains. The setting is superb, the atmosphere friendly and relaxed, the management quietly efficient. There are twenty-five rooms, with showers and air-conditioning; à la carte meals; excellent sea-food. Club membership secures a discount on the rate for the rooms as well as the facility for signing accounts which can then be settled in full at the end of your stay.

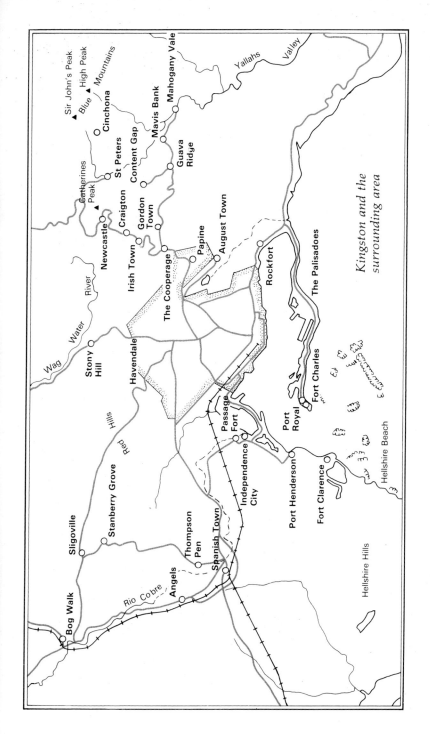

Kingston and the surrounding area

Typical Spanish Town architecture

Spanish Town

Capital of Jamaica's largest parish, St Catherine, with a population of 50 000, Spanish Town combines a vigorous present with a lively sense of past greatness. Dwellings, shops and factories straggle along the highway that leads to Kingston, Ocho Rios, Mandeville; squatters live in ramshackle huts within barriers of broken sheets of galvanised iron and farm pocket-handkerchief scraps of land; children and traders throng the streets, trucks move to the market with produce, cars and taxis hurry along the by-pass road with little thought of history and memorials. The people of Spanish Town, however, treasure their city's past. They know that today's animation and bustle are repeated in every Jamaican town, but that no other city in the Commonwealth Caribbean is as rich in historic buildings and records as theirs is.

The story begins in 1534 when Spanish colonists abandoned their first capital city, New Seville, a mile west of St Anns Bay, and moved to Spanish Town, which they called Villa de la Vega, The City of the Plain. As was the custom of all Spanish colonists, they planned a city around a central square, erected administrative buildings and a church, on whose foundations the present Cathedral stands, and also built a Franciscan monastery. The names of some of the city streets remind us of the church and the monks: White Church Street, Red Church Street, Monk Street, for example.

The site was well-chosen. The Rio Cobre provided water, the surrounding land was fertile, and an inland location gave some protection from pirates; not completely, however, for three English 'gentlemen adventurers' attacked it: Anthony Shirley in 1597, Newport in 1603, Jackson in 1640. These were damaging but temporary set-backs. Finally, in 1655 an English invading force landed at Passage Fort, by the mouth of the Rio Cobre, took the city, and made it the capital of their new colony.

For two centuries Spanish Town was Jamaica. The Governor lived there, the Supreme Court sat there, and the Council and Assembly met there to enact the laws by which the island was governed.

Lady Nugent tells of her arrival in 1805.

*I was received at the entrance to Kings House by Lord
Balcarres, some of the members of the Council and
Assembly, and the gentlemen of his own family, all with
yellow wrinkled faces. . . .*

*Up at 6 o'clock and much amused till 8 (when we
breakfasted) at seeing the black population and the odd
appearance of everything from my windows. The Kings
House, which is now our residence, is a large brick
building of two stories high, forming one side of a square;
opposite is the House of Assembly; the other two sides are
formed by a Guard House and Public Buildings. Our
apartments are very spacious but very dirty . . .*

A handsome building, the Kings House was completed about
1762, and it remained the Governor's residence up to 1872,
when the capital was moved to Kingston. In 1925 much of old
Kings House was destroyed by fire, the facade alone being
preserved. Within the stables, which have been reconditioned,
is a Folk Museum, part of a project for establishing a cultural
centre at the site.

The Spaniards laid out the square, but no trace of their
buildings remains. Rodney's memorial stands on the northern
side of the square, alongside the island's record office; just
behind is a modern building that houses the Archives, a notable
collection of papers, including some that date back to the period
of the American War of Independence and bear the signatures
of Washington, Jefferson and others. On the east side of the
square is the House of Assembly, which is now used as a
school.

The other building of greatest historical value is the
Cathedral, which stands on the site of the Spanish Chapel of the
Red Cross which was destroyed by the English invaders. The
walls are covered with monuments, some of them by the
outstanding sculptors of their day; the most notable is that to
the Earl and Countess of Effingham, a work of flowing grace
and beauty.

The first government archivist, Clinto Black, has written an
interesting and comprehensive guide to the City of Spanish
Town. Those who plan visiting the old capital will find this little
book invaluable.

Kingston-based tours

Being the island's capital, Kingston is well-served with roads and air-services. As from the hub of a wheel, highways extend east, west and to the north, providing linkages with all the resort areas. A visitor has many options: a day or more in Ocho Rios or Port Antonio, in Mandeville, Negril, Montego Bay; at Bath or the Milk River Spa; half a day in Spanish Town or Port Royal; a picnic on the Hellshire Beach; an excursion to Blue Mountain Peak; a weekend at Pine Grove in the Blue Mountain range; a tour of the coffee country around Mavis Bank; an afternoon's drive to Newcastle, 3700 feet above Kingston yet only an hour away by car; a picnic at Castleton Gardens in the valley of the Wag Water River; a tour of Spanish Town and the Bog Walk Gorge, returning by way of the Red Hills.

One's interests help toward a decision as to which options to select. Often it is possible to combine the present with the past, by including Port Royal, Spanish Town and Port Henderson on the way to the Hellshire Beach. Nature lovers, especially gardeners and botanists, will find the Botanical Gardens of absorbing interest. The mountains minister to most of us, lifting us out of ourselves with panoramic views of the Liguanea Plains, Kingston harbour, the magnificent Yallahs Valley and the Peak.

The tour desk in the hotel, the hotel staff and any of the Jamaica Tourist Board offices or tour operators can provide information and give advice. Also, consider the options for getting around: whether to rent a car or join two or three other visitors in hiring a car or a limousine or joining a group travelling by mini-bus.

Since there are so many options it is not possible to describe each route in detail. There are however, a few tours that have a special appeal for lovers of the sea, of gardens, of mountain country, of hiking and camping.

Hellshire Beach Within easy reach of Kingston, Hellshire Beach offers swimming and snorkeling, with a sparkling beach; it is very popular with Kingstonians who for generations were barred from the beach by wild scrub and hostile cactus country. Those of us who lived in Kingston got into the habit of thinking that good swimming and white-sand beaches were two hours away on the north coast, when they were actually on our doorstep. There is a good route which brings together the past and present. Take the road that leads along the Kingston waterfront from Breezy Castle to the foreshore road, Marcus Garvey Drive and the Causeway to Portmore and Port Henderson. The narrow crowded lanes and old wharves of downtown Kingston have been replaced by boulevards and open spaces, so that now Kingston can enjoy its splendid waterfront. In contrast, Port Henderson speaks of the days of Nelson and Rodney. The latter had his look-out in the hills above the port. The old houses have been restored, and one can recapture the charm and graciousness of the stonework and wooden beams. Then go on to the beach. Return by way of the Caymanas Race Course and The Ferry.

Castleton Botanical Gardens   Jamaica has a priceless heritage in its botanic gardens at Bath, Cinchona, Castleton and the Hope Gardens. Three of these show the influence of the famous Kew Gardens of London, for Nathaniel Wilson and Robert Thompson, who laid them out between 1869 and 1880, were trained at Kew. Each garden has its own individuality, through differences in temperature, rainfall and altitude.

The Castleton Gardens cover fifteen acres in the Wag Water Gorge, nineteen miles from Kingston on the Junction Road. At Hope the average annual rainfall is forty-five inches; at Castleton it is a hundred and fifteen inches, so *ixora*, azaleas and *dracaena* flourish. Flowering trees fill the place with colour throughout most of the year. Tree ferns, a lily pond, many varieties of palms, towering graceful trees, lawns, and the sound of the river, combine to make this a place of quiet beauty. The guide who takes you around is sure to show you one of the curiosities of the garden, the trap door spider.

On the return trip it is worth taking one of the side roads that branch off from the A3 at Stony Hill; either the Old Stony Hill road on the right, or the road on the left that runs along one of the mountain ridges overlooking Kingston. From either of these there are extensive views of the Liguanea Plain and Kingston Harbour.

The Blue Mountains

Pine Grove, owned and run by Ronnie and Marcia Thwaites, is the best base from which to explore the old coffee country of Jamaica, to visit the garden at Cinchona, to climb Blue Mountain Peak. Leave Kingston by the Hope Road or Old Hope Road, and continue beyond Papine by a road that runs alongside the Hope River to Gordon Town. The first famous botanical garden of Jamaica was established nearby at Spring Garden by Hinton East. This supplied the island with a variety of plants and fruit trees that were imported during the last quarter of the 18th century.

At Gordon Town, by the police station, take the road that branches right to Guava Ridge and Mavis Bank. Guava Ridge is the home of one of Jamaica's most highly acclaimed products, the Old Jamaica Liqueurs, produced and bottled by Ian Sangster, a Scotsman who built his factory at World's End, made Jamaica his home, and provided her with a valuable resource. Mr Sangster welcomes visitors. They are invited to tour the factory which is on five levels, to sample the liqueurs and to enjoy the view of Newcastle from the terrace.

Pine Grove Hotel is near the junction at the bus station beyond World's End. The main road leads on to Mavis Bank. The road that branches left climbs up to the hotel, which has a number of chalets equipped with facilities for self-catering. The atmosphere is informal and helpful without ever being intrusive.

Those who wish to see the old coffee country of Jamaica and to visit Cinchona should follow a route leading to Valda, Content Gap and Clydesdale, formerly a coffee plantation, now a forestry station. The plant was introduced into the island in 1728, but the industry did not develop until the last quarter of that century, when Britain reduced its excise duties on coffee and the Haitian revolution practically destroyed that country's export trade. A mile or so from Content Gap there is one of the best known of the coffee Great Houses of that period, Charlottenberg.

Cinchona is four miles from Clydesdale. Those who take the stiff uphill walk to the Gardens, or who choose to follow the rough road by way of Westphalia, will find an ample reward awaiting them.

The gardens are named after the cinchona tree, the bark of which was a source of quinine. The tree was introduced from Peru by Nathaniel Wilson and plants were supplied to private owners for cultivation, the Government providing them with large tracts of mountain land on easy terms. At first the project made money, but the price of the bark fell and exportation came to an end.

Aimee Webster, in her book *Caribbean Gardening*, gives a vivid picture of the gardens.

Snow in a tropical garden! So seem the frosts of white alyssum that edge formal beds of white narcissi at Cinchona. A scheme of bold white and green is the great lawn bordered by white roses and white azaleas along white gravel walks... Spice laden pinks, the mingled odours of violet, nicotina, honeysuckle pervade Cinchona Gardens. In wooded sections the aromas of camphor, cinnamon and pine are pungent. Beneath magnolia and

*rhododendron in March until early June blue agapanthus
and pink belladonna stand.... Heliotrope and hydrangea
grow profusely.... Cowslips and field daisies are wild.
Bright as new copper pennies are Australian poppies....
Despite the glory of colour, the immediate impression is
one of countless tones of green: green of bracken, silky
oak, cork, fir....*

From the gardens it is possible to pick out St Johns Peak to the
north, and the main range of the Blue Mountains from the
garden's Panoramic Walk.

There is evidence of an expanding coffee industry. This was
spearheaded by pioneers such as Keble Munn, who has his
coffee factory at Mavis Bank, and by the Government of
Jamaica. The number of coffee planters has increased, many of
them being smallholders who cultivate the coffee and then take
it to be processed at a central factory. Notable too is the
development which is being undertaken by the Japanese. In

1981 they bought Craigton Great House near Irish Town and they are pushing ahead energetically with extensive plantings of coffee on the northern slopes beyond Hardwar Gap.

So many places deserve a visit that it is not possible to name them all. Hikers and nature lovers are advised to make contact with the Government of Jamaica's Forestry Department for information about camping sites and forest reserves. For example, those visiting Newcastle can include the Hollywell Natural Forest, on the slopes around Hardwar Gap. The Forestry Department has a two-bedroom house at Clydesdale which can be leased, but the tenant must provide for himself.

The Peak

The trip is not difficult, provided it is carefully planned beforehand. The Pine Grove Hotel is a good base from which to start. Proceed to Guava Ridge, and take the Mavis Bank road which leads down through pinewoods to the Falls River and Mavis Bank. Munn's Mavis Bank Central Coffee Factory processes the coffee brought in by more than 3000 smallholders. Visitors are welcome.

Proceed from Mavis Bank to Mahogany Vale and Hagley Gap, and by a rough dirt road on the left to Fern Hill, then to Whitfield Hall, the last dwelling house on the way up to the Peak. Hikers usually overnight here, and then set off early in the morning on a three-hour walk up a steep track, making their way through mist and through elfin woodland which starts at about 5000 feet, and through scrub to a dome rather than a peak.

'. . . a little baldish flat of grass scrubbed with bilberry and blackberry bushes . . .

If the dawn were clear . . . the innocence of daybreak revealed the island like a cut beryl set in a glassy sea. The sharp ranges were of precious stone. The rivers lay veiled like opal serpents. Port Antonio shone in the ring of its harbor . . . far away to the north-east the thin lake line of Cuba was steady against the paler blue of sea and sky.

But try for a clear dawn. Kenneth Pringle, from whom I have quoted, says he only had four fine days out of a fortnight. The locals can best advise on what preparation to make and what months are best for making the trip. Here are two useful addresses:

The Jamaica Government Forests Department,
144 Constant Spring Road,
Kingston 10
tel: (305)-924-2497/2554.

The Jamaica Camping and Hiking Association,
PO Box 216,
Kingston 7
tel: (305)-927-5409.

The office is at the top of Jacks Hill, four miles up the Jacks Hill Road from the Barbican area; 5 minutes by car. There is a bus service: Bus 12.

Hotels and guest houses, Kingston

Beverley Cliff Guest House   200 Mountain View Avenue
Kingston 6; (809)-92-70951   (C)
9 rooms, 22 beds: single $12; double $9 EP; private bath/shower; air-conditioning; swimming pool.
The Courtleigh   31 Trafalgar Road, Kingston 10
(809)-92-68174/8   (B)
34 rooms, 50 beds: rates on application; private bath/shower; air-conditioning; cottages; 10% added for gratuities; restaurant; night club/discotheque; room service; tennis.
Hotel Four Seasons   18 Ruthven Road, Kingston 10
(809)-92-68805/60682   (C)
39 rooms, 78 beds: single $32–$40; double $17.50–$25 EP; private bath/shower; air-conditioning; 10% added for gratuities; restaurant.
Indies Hotel   6 Holborn Road, Kingston 10;
(809)-92-60989/62952   (C)
16 rooms, 28 beds: single $17–$32; double $13.50–$18.50 EP; private bath/shower; air-conditioning; 5% added for gratuities; restaurant.
Mayfair   4 West Kings House Close, Box 163, Kingston 10
(809)-92-61610   (C)
30 rooms, 60 beds: single $30–$40; double $17.50–$22.50 EP; private bath/shower; air-conditioning; swimming pool; 10% added for gratuities; restaurant; room service.
New Kingston Hotel   Box 83, Kingston 5. (809)-92-65430
Telex: 2152   (B)
190 rooms, 380 beds: single $75–$85; double $42.50–$47.50 EP; private bath/shower; air-conditioning; swimming pool; 10% added

for gratuities; restaurant; resort shops; beauty parlour; room service; telephone in all rooms; tennis; tour desk.

Hotel Oceana, Kingston   Box 986, Kingston (809)-92-20920/5
Telex: 2230 Kinja   **(B)**
150 rooms, 300 beds: single $68–$78; double $39–$44 EP; private bath/shower; air-conditioning; swimming pool; 10% added for gratuities; restaurant; resort shops; beauty parlour; room service; telephone in all rooms; tour desk.

Olympia Residential Hotel   Old Hope Road, Kingston 6
(809)-92-79851   **(C)**
19 rooms, 35 beds: single $22; double $12.50 EP; private bath/shower; air-conditioning; 10% added for gratuities; room service; telephone in all rooms.

Sandhurst Guest House   70 Sandhurst Crescent, Kingston 6
(809)-92-77239/78244   **(C)**
40 rooms, 65 beds: single $20–$26; double $14–$18 EP; private bath/shower; partial air-conditioning; swimming pool; 10% added for gratuities; restaurant; room service; beauty parlour; tour desk.

Sutton Place   11 Ruthven Road, Kingston 10
(809)-92-62297   **(C)**
30 rooms, 60 beds; single $40–$70; double $20–$35 EP; private bath/shower; air-conditioning; swimming pool; restaurant; room service: telephone in all rooms.

Terra Nova   17 Waterloo Road, Kingston 10
(809)-92-62211/69334; Telex 2194 MANCOM JA   **(B)**
34 rooms, 64 beds; single $60; double $32.50 EP; private bath/shower; air-conditioning; swimming pool; 10% added for gratuities; restaurant; room service; telephone in all rooms.

196

14 The South Coast, Mandeville and Milk River Spa

General information

It's more than an area – it's a region as large as Curaçao or Aruba, extending along the south coast for eighty miles from Milk River and Calabash Bay through Alligator Pond to Savanna-la-Mar, capital of Westmoreland. It reaches inland to include two places of special interest, Mandeville, twenty miles north of Alligator Pond, and the Milk River Spa, six miles inland from the mouth of the Milk River, and fifty miles from Kingston. The key points are Mandeville, the Milk River Spa, Treasure Beach near Alligator Pond, and Bluefields to the west.

Visitors are just discovering the South Coast, especially those in search of a natural holiday, a vacation with the family on quiet beaches, a health vacation, a fishing and snorkeling holiday. There are also many who choose a combination holiday, getting the best of both worlds by enjoying the more sophisticated north coast and the more rural south coast.

The first impression is of space, because the coastal plain is wider than on the north coast; but the physical configuration is the same, so that you climb from the plain up a series of escarpments to green inland terraces and plateaux. At some points the ridge ends abruptly at the shore, as at Lover's Leap which stands 1600 feet above the sea. At Swamp there is a fantasy-land of lagoons; at Lacovia a two-mile long bamboo avenue; and from the top of Spur Tree Hill a view of the Westmoreland Plain.

Because the area is large, with many attractions and limited accommodation, visitors are advised to consult with the

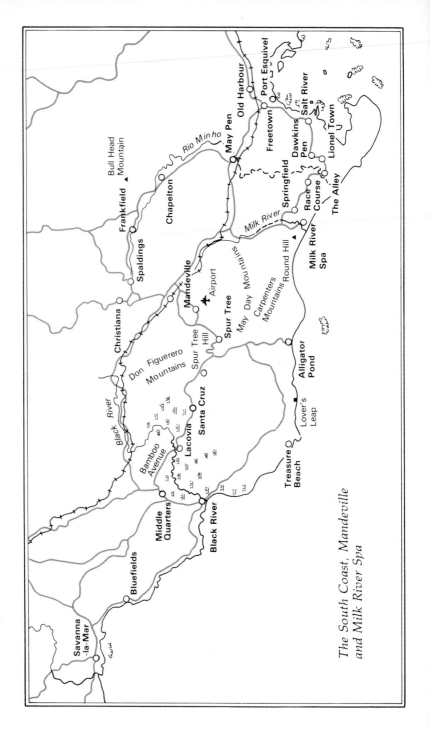

The South Coast, Mandeville and Milk River Spa

Jamaica Tourist Board and with the South Coast Marketing Company (SCMC), which has an office at the Hotel Astra in Mandeville. The SCMC was set up by the Government to attract visitors to the area and to assist them. SCMC offers combination packages, with some or all of the various bases included in the package. A choice of tours is added to each option. Accommodation is available in villas and hotels.

Mandeville

Colonial governors served a five-year term of office before stepping up to some larger part of the empire or stepping down from the feathered plumes and ceremonial swords of their office to the sombre felt hats and folded umbrellas of retirement; a difficult and traumatic experience.

But the Duke of Manchester broke all records for ceremonial longevity. He governed Jamaica for nineteen years. While he was Governor, planters and merchants who lived in outlying parts of the parishes of Westmoreland, Vere and Clarendon got together and urged the creation of a new parish, with an administrative centre within easier reach, an important consideration in an age of horse-drawn carriages. Following the example of Solomon, the Duke and the House of Assembly carved pieces out of the older parishes of St Elizabeth, Vere and Clarendon to create a new parish, which was named Manchester, after the Duke. The Duke's heir was Lord Mandeville, so the capital of the new parish was named after him.

Up to the 1950's Manchester produced cattle, pimento, citrus and vegetables. Mandeville was the attractive social and commercial centre not only of the parish but also of a large section of central Jamaica. Being 2000 feet above sea-level it has a near-perfect climate, with a temperature rarely higher than 85°F in the summer, or lower than 55°F in the depth of winter. The night sky is brilliant with stars throughout the year, so much so that years ago two celebrated American astronomers, Hamilton and William Pickering, set up their telescopes on the edge of the town.

Having secured a parish and a capital town, the Manchester people started to clamour that Mandeville, with its climate, its efficient communication network and its central location, should be made the summer capital of Jamaica. They pressed their case when Governor Sir Hugh Foot, greatly loved by all Jamaicans, visited Mandeville in the 1950's. But Hugh Foot, (now Lord Caradon) was better versed in holy writ than were the petitioners. Resisting the pressure, he reminded them of the Bibilical injunction, 'Thou shalt not suffer thy Foot to be moved.'

In the 1950's the character of this placid country town, built in 1816, with an English style village green, Parish Church and Court House and with shops and offices lining the other sides of the green, began to change. The town and its people were sitting in the centre of Jamaica's 'red earth' or bauxite country. Alcan Jamaica, one of the pioneer companies of Jamaica's bauxite industry set up its offices a mile away from the village green, and built its Kirkvine works, to process bauxite into aluminium – a pioneering effort that none of the other bauxite companies attempted at that time – five miles away, at Kendall. Modern residences and shopping centres began to spread across the pastures. Manchester and Jamaica had gained an industrial base for their economy. Some years later the Kaiser Company set up its headquarters at Spur Tree, five miles to the south. Today, Mandeville draws its strength from agriculture and industry. The town has no ghettos. Its people are vigorous and civic-minded, representative of the townsfolk of many of the upland towns of Jamaica such as Spaldings, Christiana and Browns Town.

Mandeville has an airport which is used by TransJamaica, Jamaica Wings and small aircraft. It is near the Kirkvine Works of Alcan and five miles from the town.

Come and keep company with us again

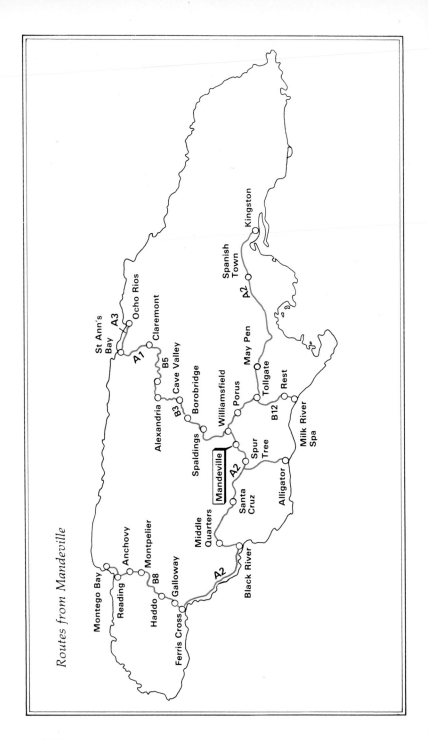

Routes from Mandeville

Mandeville is linked by road with Montego Bay and Western Jamaica, Ocho Rios and the north coast, Kingston, the Milk River Spa and the South Coast. The chief routes are shown on the map.

1 Mandeville to Montego Bay by way of A2 leading west, through Santa Cruz, Middle Quarters, Black River, Bluefields, Ferris Cross, then north by the B8 by way of Galloway, Haddo, Montpelier, Anchovy and Reading to Montego Bay: 86 miles, about 3 hours.

2 Mandeville to Kingston by A2, by way of Williamsfield, Porus, Toll Gate, May Pen, Old Harbour, Spanish Town: 61 miles, about 2 hours.

3 Mandeville to Milk River Spa by A2, by way of Williamsfield, Porus, Toll Gate; turn right on to B12 by way of St Jago, Rest to the Milk River Spa: 28 miles; about 1½ hours.

4 Mandeville to Alligator Pond by way of A2 to Spur Tree, Gutters, turn left on road to Alligator Pond by way of Watsons Hill and Rowes Corner: about 23 miles, 1½ hours.

5 Mandeville to Ocho Rios by B5 north by way of Williamsfield, up Shooters Hill through Walderston, Spaldings, then north through Borobridge, Cave Valley, by B3 to Alexandria, then east through Alva, Albion, Bonneville, Claremont, then north by the A1 to St Ann's Bay and then east by the A3 to Ocho Rios: 65 miles; about 3 hours.

Milk River Spa

Recently, at the invitation of the Government of Jamaica, a team of consultants from West Germany visited the island and analysed the waters of fifteen mineral springs. Their report showed that the island has in most of these springs a very valuable and hitherto neglected resource. The three major spas are those at Milk River, at Bath in the parish of St Thomas and at Sans Souci on the north coast near Ocho Rios. These are being developed.

The report confirmed earlier analyses of the water of the Milk River Spa, that therapeutically it was more efficacious than the waters of Baden or Vichy and that its radio-activity was fifty times greater than theirs. Many Jamaicans suffering from rheumatic complaints and arthritis have found the Spa highly beneficial.

The Milk River is a slow-moving stream that flows through flat land, part of Jamaica's largest plain which stretches from Kingston west into the parish of Clarendon, and to the Manchester hills. Clarendon, one of the island's largest parishes, has an area of 487 square miles. In the north, around Frankfield and Chapelton, are the mountains. The most conspicuous is the Bull Head Mountain, 3600 feet high, standing at the centre of Jamaica. The chief physical feature is the Round Hill in Vere.

The plain has some tobacco and sisal, cattle and sugar-cane, and one of Jamaica's largest sugar factories, Monymusk. The north has citrus and a variety of foodcrops.

The large expanse of flat land, the fertile soil and excellent climate of the north attracted settlers from the very beginning of English colonisation in 1655.

The healing waters of the Spa will attract more and more visitors as it becomes widely known. Visitors will enjoy exploring upper Clarendon for the beauty of its landscape, its excellent climate and its historic associations.

Old plantations tour

This tour can be made from the Milk River Spa, and also from Kingston, Mandeville, Ocho Rios or Falmouth on the north coast. Start from the Spa, and proceed by way of Milk River and the B12 through Springfield, Race Course, Alley, Lionel Town, Dawkins Pen and Salt River to join the A2 at Freetown, and then continue to Old Harbour. Alley Church, built in 1715, has some old monuments. The Salt River is used for transporting sugar and Port Esquivel, near Old Harbour, is a bauxite port built for shipping Alcan's alumina.

From Old Harbour onwards let Leonard Sutton be your guide. One of his ancestors was among the first English settlers. His descendants run the gracious property Marshalls Pen, near Mandeville, with three hundred acres of cattle country, hiking trails, horseback riding, a bird sanctuary, a wild garden and a charming Great House with valuable antique furniture. Marshalls Pen has limited accommodation for guests. Those who love nature and history will find it a refreshing, hospitable place.

After leaving Old Harbour this route leads through the part of the country which was settled shortly after the conquest of the island in 1655 by Englishmen of historic fame such as Colbeck, Morant, Pennant, Collier, Long, Wildman, Sutton, Dawkins, Beckford, Bright, Penrhyn, Gale, Sinclair, Morgan, and in many instances their names are still preserved in the names of the properties they owned.

The first point of interest is the ruin of Colbeck Castle. This is the only moat-surrounded fortress in the island, and was erected by Colonel Colbeck who came to Jamaica with Penn and Venables at the time of the conquest (1655) . . . . Next on the route comes Sevens Plantation, settled by Anthony Collier who was member of the first Council (1671), then Longville, settled by Samuel Long who also came with Penn and Venables in 1655. He found on the banks of the Rio Minho, which flows through the property, basins where the Indians and later the Spaniards washed for gold. A mile or so further on and skirting the river the old sugar works of Moore's Hall are to be seen. . . .

Retreat is the next point of interest. It belonged to the wealthy Beckford Family, one of whom was Lord Mayor of London. This was also a sugar plantation. Some copper mining has been done on the property.

Leaving Retreat, the Bull Head, the highest point in this particular mountain range, soon comes into view . . . it marks the centre of the island. Kellets, famed for its beautiful cut stone ruins, which lie beneath, was settled by Moses Kellet. . . .

On approaching Rock River village the fine aqueduct and works of the sugar estate Rock River, with its charming surroundings of hills, valley, river and tobacco fields, present an extraordinarily beautiful view. A mile further on the Rio Minho is crossed . . . and the road leads on past the sugar works of Low Ground which at one time was owned by the Wildman family of Chilham Castle, Kent. A lovely view of the Minho valley is obtained from

*the road above the works, also of Suttons Plantation,
formerly owned by Colonel Thomas Sutton who
commanded the Militia and repulsed the French Admiral
Du Casse in 1694 at Carlisle Bay. The property eventually
came into the possession of his kinsman Henry Dawkins
whose crest is carved on the doorway of the old boiling
house. The motto is 'Strike, Dawkins, strike, the Devil's in
the hemp.'*

*Leaving Chapelton, the route passes through the sugar
plantations of Danks and Savoy, formerly in the possession
of the Beckford Family. It is worthy of note that Colonel
Beckford, who lived at Danks, was appointed to allot land
to form the city of Kingston after the great earthquake of
1692. Beckford Street, Kingston, was named after him in
1702. Morgans Valley, close by, was in the possession of
the famous buccanneer Morgan, who later in life was
knighted and became Governor of Jamaica in 1678.*

Treasure Beach, near Alligator Pond, is used by SCMC as a
centre for the surrounding area, including Great Bay and
Calabash Bay. Improvements are now being made to the
Treasure Beach Hotel, which has fourteen rooms, a swimming
pool and a restaurant. In addition the Company has identified
thirty villas suitable for guests, some with swimming pools,
some fronting on the ocean.

Bluefields/Belmont, on the Westmoreland coast, eleven miles
east of Savanna-la-Mar, and fifty-six miles from Mandeville by
way of Black River. Like Negril Bay, Bluefields was often used
by sailing ships in search of safe anchorage and a plentiful
supply of fresh water. The records of Spanish Jamaica show
that there was a small settlement here, called Oristan. In 1670
Henry Morgan, Admiral and Commander in Chief, collected a
fleet of thirty-six ships, set sail from Bluefields, landed on the
Isthmus of Panama, hacked his way through malaria-infested
tropical jungle for eight days, captured and sacked Panama,
and returned to Port Royal with a rich cargo of silver, gold,
jewellery and rich vestments. The total value amounted to
750 000 pieces of eight.

Mandeville

Hotel Astra Box 60, Mandeville: (809)-962-3265/3377   (C)
22 rooms, 40 beds: single $55–$75; double $55–$75 EP; private bath/
shower; pool; fishing; golf; 10% added for gratuities; beauty parlour;
tennis; horseback riding; family-run hotel.
Mandeville Hotel Box 78, Mandeville: (809)-962-2460   (C)
66 rooms, 132 beds: single $20–$49; double $13–$34 EP; private bath/
shower; partial air-conditioning; pool; golf; both golf and tennis can
be arranged at the Mandeville Club.

The sun sets at the end of a perfect day

Further reading

Also published by Macmillan Caribbean

By Sir Philip Sherlock
(with J. Parry)   *A Short History of the West Indies*
Norman Manley: A Biography
(with Hilary Sherlock)   *Ears & Tails & Commonsense*
Anansi the Spider Man

F.A. Hoyos   *Barbados: The Visitor's Guide*
H.A. Fergus   *Montserrat Emerald Isle of the Caribbean*
G. Glanville   *Beaches U.S. Virgin Islands*

de Lisser   *The White Witch of Rosehall*
Floyd   *Jamaica An Island Microcosm*
Hall   *Jamaica Land We Love*

Lennox and Seddon   *Flowers of the Caribbean*
Seddon and Lennox   *Trees of the Caribbean*
Took   *Fishes of the Caribbean Reefs*
Jones and Sefton   *Marine Life of the Caribbean*

Barratt   *Grand Bahama*
Saunders   *Historic Nassau*
Albury   *Paradise Island*
Campbell   *The Ephemeral Islands*
MacLean   *Reptiles and Amphibians of the Virgin Islands*